THE ABORTION RIGHTS MOVEMENT

THE ABORTION RIGHTS MOVEMENT

OTHER BOOKS IN THE
AMERICAN SOCIAL MOVEMENTS SERIES:

AMERICAN
SOCIAL
MOVEMENTS

THE ABORTION RIGHTS MOVEMENT

Meghan Powers, *Book Editor*

Bruce Glassman, *Vice President*
Bonnie Szumski, *Publisher*
Helen Cothran, *Managing Editor*

GREENHAVEN PRESS
An imprint of Thomson Gale, a part of The Thomson Corporation

Detroit • New York • San Francisco • San Diego • New Haven, Conn.
Waterville, Maine • London • Munich

THOMSON
™
GALE

LIBRARY OF CONGRESS CATALOGING-IN-PUBLICATION DATA
The abortion rights movement / Meghan Powers, book editor.
p. cm. — (American social movements)
Includes bibliographical references and index.
ISBN 0-7377-1947-8 (lib. : alk. paper)
1. Pro-choice movement—United States—History. 2. Abortion—United States—History. I. Powers, Meghan. II. Series.
HQ767.5.U5A2653 2006
363.46'0973—dc22   2005046108

CONTENTS

Chapter 2 • THE MOVEMENT FIGHTS TO PRESERVE ABORTION

Chapter 4 • ABORTION IN THE TWENTY-FIRST CENTURY

FOREWORD

Historians Gary T. Marx and Douglas McAdam define a social movement as "organized efforts to promote or resist change in society that rely, at least in part, on noninstitutionalized forms of political action." Examining American social movements broadens and vitalizes the study of history by allowing students to observe the efforts of ordinary individuals and groups to oppose the established values of their era, often in unconventional ways. The civil rights movement of the twentieth century, for example, began as an effort to challenge legalized racial segregation and garner social and political rights for African Americans. Several grassroots organizations—groups of ordinary citizens committed to social activism—came together to organize boycotts, sit-ins, voter registration drives, and demonstrations to counteract racial discrimination. Initially, the movement faced massive opposition from white citizens, who had long been accustomed to the social standards that required the separation of the races in almost all areas of life. But the movement's consistent use of an innovative form of protest—nonviolent direct action—eventually aroused the public conscience, which in turn paved the way for major legislative victories such as the Civil Rights Act of 1964 and the Voting Rights Act of 1965. Examining the civil rights movement reveals how ordinary people can use nonstandard political strategies to change society.

Investigating the style, tactics, personalities, and ideologies of American social movements also encourages students to learn about aspects of history and culture that may receive scant attention in textbooks. As scholar Eric Foner notes, American history "has been constructed not only in congressional debates and political treatises, but also on plantations and picket lines, in parlors and bedrooms. Frederick Douglass, Eugene V. Debs, and Margaret Sanger . . . are its architects as well as Thomas Jefferson and Abraham Lincoln." While not all

American social movements garner popular support or lead to epoch-changing legislation, they each offer their own unique insight into a young democracy's political dialogue.

Each book in Greenhaven's American Social Movements series allows readers to follow the general progression of a particular social movement—examining its historical roots and beginnings in earlier chapters and relatively recent and contemporary information (or even the movement's demise) in later chapters. With the incorporation of both primary and secondary sources, as well as writings by both supporters and critics of the movement, each anthology provides an engaging panoramic view of its subject. Selections include a variety of readings, such as book excerpts, newspaper articles, speeches, manifestos, literary essays, interviews, and personal narratives. The editors of each volume aim to include the voices of movement leaders and participants as well as the opinions of historians, social analysts, and individuals who have been affected by the movement. This comprehensive approach gives students the opportunity to view these movements both as participants have experienced them and as historians and critics have interpreted them.

Every volume in the American Social Movements series includes an introductory essay that presents a broad historical overview of the movement in question. The annotated table of contents and comprehensive index help readers quickly locate material of interest. Each selection is preceded by an introductory paragraph that summarizes the article's content and provides historical context when necessary. Several other research aids are also present, including brief excerpts of supplementary material, a chronology of major events pertaining to the movement, and an accessible bibliography.

The Greenhaven Press American Social Movements series offers readers an informative introduction to some of the most fascinating groups and ideas in American history. The contents of each anthology provide a valuable resource for general readers as well as for enthusiasts of American political science, history, and culture.

INTRODUCTION

An Issue of
Social Equality

From its earliest days, the abortion rights movement saw itself not just as a movement to ensure legal abortion. Its
founders, most of whom were activists in the feminist movement, saw abortion as central to women's pursuit of social
equality. In their view, women could never achieve equality or
fully realize their civil and human rights while men or even
other women could dictate choices involving that most personal
of decisions: when to have a child.

At the 1969 founding of NARAL (now known as the National Abortion Rights Action League), feminist Betty Friedan
strongly urged her colleagues to speak clearly on this subject.
She proposed that the NARAL charter begin by "asserting the
right of a woman to control her own body and reproductive
process as her inalienable, human, civil right, not to be denied
or abridged by the state, or any man."[1]

RIGHTS AND PRINCIPLES

The abortion rights movement still holds to this view. Its members see a clear connection between the ultimate goal of social
equality and, in Friedan's words, a woman's ability "to control her
reproductive process."[2] In this context, abortion is but one issue—
albeit the hottest of hot-button issues—in a broader debate. "We
are not debating abortion," writes Don Sloan, a physician and assistant editor of the monthly periodical *Political Affairs*. "We are
debating rights. Rights, not morals; rights, not ethics."[3]

Ironically, many members of the anti-abortion movement also
see abortion as a civil rights issue. But the issue, as they see it, is
not about civil rights or social justice for women. Rather, they

see legalized abortion as a threat to America's longstanding legal principles and democratic political ideals. "Abortion...cuts to the heart of America's claim to being a law-governed democracy, in which equality before the law is a fundamental principle of justice," one writer states in the bimonthly journal *Society*. A law that permits abortion, abortion opponents believe, is akin to the laws that once allowed exclusion from many settings based on race. "Thus," the *Society* article states, "the abortion issue is the crucial civil rights issue of our time."[4]

Both sides in this debate frequently call on images of an earlier time, when the nation's laws sanctioned differences in how people were treated depending on their race. Henry Morgentaler, founding president of the Humanist Association of Canada, contends that abortion—or more broadly, reproductive freedom—is essential for social justice and the "emancipation" of women.

In the publication *Free Inquiry* he writes: "Women cannot achieve their full potential unless they have freedom to control their bodies, to control their reproductive capacity. Unless they have access to safe abortions to correct the vagaries of biological accidents, they cannot pursue careers, they cannot be equal to men, they cannot avail themselves of the various opportunities theoretically open to all members of our species. The emancipation of women is not possible without reproductive freedom."[5]

A BROADER CONTEXT

How these ideas—abortion and social equality—became so intertwined can be understood in the context of the feminist movement's early years. In the 1960s and early 1970s (before the legalization of abortion in 1973), feminists "saw themselves as part of a larger movement that was challenging basic social, economic, and political institutions,"[6] writes author Suzanne Staggenborg. One of the institutions seen as damaging to women (and by extension, children and families) was the traditional health care system. That system did not adequately serve women and their families, in the view of feminists. It offered limited access to quality health care, minimal say in health care decisions, and a traditional doctor-patient relationship modeled on a patriarchal hierarchy.

In short, the women's movement saw a need for broad change in the area of health care. Abortion fit into the larger agenda but "legal abortion was not an end in itself," Staggenborg writes. Instead, it was viewed as "part of a broader fight for 'women's control of their bodies' and a responsive health care system."[7]

In a sense, neither fight has been won. Efforts to restructure the health care system are ongoing, and abortion, though legal, remains one of the most contentious (and unsettled) issues of our time. For the abortion rights movement, then, abortion still stands at the center of an ongoing debate over social equality for women. As Beverly Wildung Harrison, a professor of Christian Ethics at Union Theological Seminary in New York, writes: "Genuine choice with respect to procreative power (not simply choice for the sake of choice) is a necessary condition of *any and all* women's human fulfillment. When the day comes that the decision to bear a child, for all women, is a moral choice—that is, a deliberated, thoughtful decision to act for the enhancement of our own and our society's well-being with full responsibility for all the implications of that action—then and only then, the human liberation of women will be a reality."[8]

NOTES

1. Betty Friedan, *"It Changed My Life": Writings on the Women's Movement.* New York: W.W. Norton, 1985, p. 122.

2. Friedan, *"It Changed My Life,"* p. 124.

3. Don Sloan, "Basic Issues in the Abortion Debate," *Political Affairs,* July 1999.

4. *Society,* "The America We Seek," July/August 1997.

5. Henry Morgentaler, "The Moral Case for Abortion," *Free Inquiry,* Summer 1996.

6. Suzanne Staggenborg, "Confrontation and Direct Action," in *The Pro-Choice Movement: Organization and Activism in the Abortion Conflict.* New York: Oxford US, 1991, p. 44.

7. Staggenborg, "Confrontation and Direct Action," p. 46.

8. Beverly Wildung Harrison, *Our Right to Choose: Toward a New Ethic of Abortion.* Boston, MA: Beacon Press, 1983.

CHAPTER 1

THE ORIGINS OF THE ABORTION MOVEMENT IN AMERICA

AMERICAN
SOCIAL
MOVEMENTS

Abortion in Early American Society

LAURENCE H. TRIBE

Laurence H. Tribe is a scholar and a teacher of constitutional law at Harvard University. Tribe's *Abortion: The Clash of Absolutes,* from which the following article is excerpted, analyzes the social and political components of the abortion debate starting at the founding of the nation in the late eighteenth century. He describes how abortion, which was neither prohibited nor uncommon in the late 1700s, became socially and legally unacceptable by the middle of the nineteenth century.

The regulation of abortion began in the nineteenth century along with most laws concerning women's health, but restrictive abortion laws were enacted in the mid-nineteenth century as a result of organized lobbying by the medical profession. Tribe contends that the change in the social perception of abortion was essentially due to the American Medical Association's campaign to end legal abortion starting in 1859. The medical profession used changing social and demographic forces, specifically the decreasing birth rate among native-born white women and increased birth rates of immigrant women, to awaken racist fears among Protestant middle and upper classes and dissuade abortion in Protestant communities. Tribe examines further how in its efforts to reduce abortion rates the American Medical Association used fear and humiliation, casting women who sought abortion as selfish and immoral. Essentially, Tribe argues that the medical profession shaped public opinion and the subsequent laws regarding abortion passed in the middle of the nineteenth century, some of which can still be seen today.

Laurence H. Tribe, *Abortion: The Clash of Absolutes.* New York: W.W. Norton & Company, 1990. Copyright © 1990 by W.W. Norton & Company, Inc. Reproduced by permission.

In early post-Revolution America, abortion, at least early in pregnancy, was neither prohibited nor uncommon. Each American jurisdiction—that is, each of the states—was governed by the common law, the corpus of English judge-made law that had evolved over the centuries preceding the Revolution, as supplemented by legislated laws. At the time of the Revolution and of the adoption of the United States Constitution—indeed, until 1821—no state had enacted a statute outlawing abortion.

Under common law, abortion was permitted until "quickening," the time when the first movement of the fetus was perceived by the woman. In practice this meant that abortion was unrestricted until the fourth or fifth month of pregnancy. This rule was supported by a number of rationales. For some, fetal movement signified that the fetus had a soul. For others, especially those in the medical profession, performance of an abortion before quickening was deemed to present little danger to the woman's health. At the most pragmatic level, the distinction was rooted in the scientific limitations of the time: Before quickening, no one could know for sure if a woman was pregnant. If it could not be known that a woman was pregnant, it could not be proved that an abortion had been performed and certainly not that one had been intentionally performed. The common law also provided that even when an illegal abortion was performed, the woman involved was immune from prosecution.

Because postquickening abortion was considered a crime, we know that the first American lawmakers valued fetal life. But we cannot know with certainty how high a value they put on it. During the early history of the United States abortion was at worst considered a misdemeanor offense. This may mean that society attached little moral significance or legal importance to the fetus. But it could also reflect judicial and legislative restraint in the face of great uncertainty about the existence and development of the unborn. . . .

Abortion of unwanted pregnancies apparently was not unusual in the United States during the late eighteenth and early nineteenth centuries. At the beginning of this period American attitudes toward sexuality became more liberal. Indeed, one historian, Michael Gordon, has calculated that three of ten women in late-eighteenth-century New England were pregnant at the time they married. This was more than three times the rate of pregnancy among brides a hundred years before. That there was a decline in the overall birthrate during this same period suggests an increase in the use of both birth control and abortion.

Eighteenth- and nineteenth-century American society was predominantly rural. Such societies typically value children as a source of economic strength, and the United States was no exception. For this reason abortions were sought primarily by single women. A woman generally resorted to abortion to conceal the sexual behavior that resulted in her pregnancy. Abortion as such was not perceived as a great moral issue. Abortion was the subject of debate only in terms of the illicit sexual behavior that occasioned it, behavior so harshly condemned at times that society's rebuke must have been a terrible thing for women to endure.

The regulation of abortion by statute began in America in the nineteenth century. The earliest laws were primarily about women's health Nineteenth-century abortion methods were as dangerous as one might imagine. When one considers that it was popular to administer poisons to pregnant women to induce abortion (on the dubious theory that a dosage sufficient to kill the fetus might spare the woman), it is understandable that America's first statutory abortion regulation, enacted by the state of Connecticut in 1821, prohibited only the inducement of abortion through the use of dangerous poisons.

The Connecticut statute applied, even then, only to postquickening abortions, testimony to the strength of the view that a woman should be able to end an unwanted, unconfirmed early pregnancy. Indeed, America's first abortion statutes dealt primarily with postquickening abortion. . . .

Between 1800 and 1900 the rate of fertility—the average number of children born to each woman—for white American women (the only group for which statistics are readily available) dropped almost 50 percent, from 7.04 to 3.56 children. This drop coincided with an increase in the visibility of abortion. The popular press carried advertisements for home abortifacients and remedies to relieve "menstrual blockage." These home remedies were often unsafe and ineffective and ranged from strenuous exercise to soap solutions and mild poisons to physical intrusions into the uterus. The rate of abortion increased, and by the middle of the nineteenth century there was, by some estimates, one induced abortion for every four live births.

The Role of the Medical Profession

When restrictive abortion laws were finally enacted in the United States in the mid-nineteenth century, the force behind them was neither religious belief nor a popular moral crusade. Rather, our strict abortion laws were the product of lobbying by the organized medical profession and reflected increased professionalization of the practice of medicine.

The motivations that lay behind the physicians' movement to outlaw abortion seem quite complex. "Regular" physicians—generally those who were trained in the more rigorous medical schools and who subscribed to the scientific method—were certainly concerned about the safety of abortions to the women who underwent them. In the face of a rapidly swelling number of irregular physicians and apothecaries promising miraculous abortional procedures, the profession also felt the need to police its boundaries. In part to legitimize and consolidate the medical profession, physicians were eager to halt the competition in abortion services from medical irregulars.

In the mid-nineteenth century regular physicians were the members of society most vocally committed to defending the value of human life. In 1857 Dr. Horatio Storer, a specialist in obstetrics and gynecology who was then the leading American advocate for the criminalization of abortion, launched a national drive by the ten-year-old American Medical Association (AMA) to end legal abortion. At its annual convention in 1859 the AMA called for the "general suppression" of abortions, including those performed before quickening. The physicians organized an effective media and lobbying campaign that focused on the fetus's right to life. Over time their efforts altered the prevailing attitudes about the practice in the United States. . . .

SOCIAL AND DEMOGRAPHIC FORCES

The doctors' campaign was by no means a pure question of abstract morality—for any segment of society. The movement also reflected (and appealed to) concerns spurred by a metamorphosis in the social meaning of abortion. As increasing numbers of married white middle-class Protestant women chose to interrupt pregnancies, abortion took on for powerful groups new and threatening significance.

By 1860 the birthrate among white Americans of British and northern European descent had declined significantly by comparison with that of the newly arrived, predominantly Catholic groups, in part as a result of an increased rate of abortion among the more established Americans. In 1855, for example, the birthrate among thirty- to thirty-four-year-old Irish immigrant women in Buffalo was more than twice that for native-born white Protestant women.

Doctors used the transformation in the demographics of abortion to awaken among the Protestant middle and upper classes racist fears regarding the ethnic makeup of the United States. Eugenic concerns, expressed as a fear of race suicide through the failure to have enough children, motivated and were relied upon by physicians advocating abortion restrictions. An 1865 tract by antiabortion physician Horatio Storer, for example, asserts that abortion is "infinitely more frequent among Protestant women than among Catholic." Another physician voiced concern about the threat to what he called "our most intelligent communities." Physicians at the time also expressed particular concern about abortion among women of "high repute."

Protestant fears of race suicide were far more prominent in the mid-nineteenth-century movement against abortion than was religious antiabortion sentiment of any kind. Indeed, historian Mohr concludes that such opposition to abortion as *was* expressed by Protestant clergy was motivated more by the declining birthrates of adherents than by moral opposition to the practice.

THE EARLY ROLE OF WOMEN'S CONCERNS

Declining birthrates also threatened a different kind of revolution in the social order. A central theme throughout the history of abortion in America is that women who are able to control their reproductive destinies gain freedom to pursue personal missions other than the traditional one in the home. The physicians' campaign for abortion regulation urged that abortion posed a threat to traditional sex roles.

An 1871 report of the American Medical Association Committee on Criminal Abortion is a disturbing example of this appeal. This report describes the woman seeking an abortion as "unmindful of the course marked out for her by Providence" and characterizes her as selfish and immoral. The report reflects a vision in which female sexuality cannot honorably be divorced from the traditional role of wife and mother: "She yields to the pleasures—but shrinks from the pains and responsibilities of maternity. . . . Let not the husband of such a wife flatter himself that he possesses her affection. Nor can she in turn ever merit even the respect of a virtuous husband. She sinks into old age like a withered tree, stripped of its foliage; with the stain of blood upon her soul, she dies without the hand of affection to smooth her pillow." What is most striking about this vision is the attempt to pit husbands, who must often have participated in decisions to terminate pregnancy, against their wives.

The fears of dislocation in traditional family structures were no doubt reinforced by an increase in the percentage of women who worked. The urbanization of America during this period increased the number of working-class women forced to supplement their husbands' wages with incomes of their own. The dramatically transformed terms in which abortion was depicted and the altered terms through which the woman who would choose an abortion was described reflect a graphic, sometimes desperate effort to reassert traditional social control and male dominance.

Intriguingly, abortion rights, despite this link to the control of women by men, were not really on the agenda of the early feminists. For them questions of reproduction were primarily about avoiding death in childbirth. To this end they advocated "voluntary motherhood," primarily through sexual abstinence. Within the context of nineteenth-century morality, the feminists attempted to seize a high ground of sorts by arguing that women were by nature morally superior; women could oppose abortion because unlike men, women were thought willing to abstain from sex and were viewed to be by nature nurturing.

THE NINETEENTH-CENTURY LAWS

The nineteenth-century physicians' campaign mobilized public opinion. Within less than two decades, more than forty antiabortion statutes had been passed in the United States. The structure of these laws tells the story of their purpose. In general, mid-to-late-nineteenth-century abortion legislation abandoned the distinction between quick and nonquick fetuses. Like some earlier laws that had been supported by regular physicians, these statutes tended to have exceptions for "therapeutic" abortion. Typically abortion would be permitted when necessary *in the opinion of a physician* to preserve the life of the woman. (Ten states required the concurrence of a second physician.)

The regular physicians succeeded in their movement to obtain control of the practice of abortion; the social metamorphosis of the abortion question into a matter of "medical judgment" had taken hold. The laws reflecting and reinforcing this metamorphosis sent out a powerful signal about the role of the medical profession.

Laws dating from this period may appear familiar. Although the issue is clouded by subsequent enactments that worked to repeal inconsistent earlier laws, versions of these laws arguably remain on the books in more than thirty states today.

African American Women's Activism

LORETTA J. ROSS

Activist and scholar Loretta J. Ross has committed her life's work to fighting social injustices and inequalities. She is the founder and executive director of the National Center for Human Rights Education and has worked with the National Black Women's Health Project and the National Organization for Women. She has mobilized women of color for reproductive rights marches and demonstrations and coordinated events such as the 1987 National Conference on Women of Color and Reproductive Rights. In the following excerpt, Ross examines the history of African American women's participation in the abortion rights movement. She argues that African American women have always been committed to abortion rights, and their influence should not be ignored.

Long before the women's liberation movement or any formal abortion rights organizations, African American women slaves were taking control of their own fertility through the use of contraception and the practice of abortion. In the early twentieth century the African American community mobilized, and a black women's club movement began. These clubs had thousands of members and were all over the United States, providing a forum to discuss black women's sexuality. Ross articulates that the black women's club movement cast African American women as early activists who would go on to become integral members of the birth control and abortion rights movements.

B efore the Civil War, almost 20 percent of the total United States population consisted of African-American slaves. Plantation owners tried to keep knowledge of birth control and abortion away from both slaves and white women to maintain

Loretta J. Ross, "African-American Women and Abortion," *Abortion Wars: A Half Century of Struggle, 1950–2000,* edited by Rickie Solinger. Berkeley: University of California Press, 1998. Copyright © 1998 by The Regents of the University of California. Reproduced by permission.

the system of white supremacy used to justify slavery and to increase their investments in human chattel. In addition to the rape of slave women by slave masters to increase the number of children, breeding techniques included giving pregnant slave women lighter workloads and more rations to increase their willingness to have children. Punitive measures were also used: infertile women were treated "like barren sows and . . . passed from one unsuspecting buyer to the next."

African Americans covertly used contraceptives and abortions to resist slavery. Often they employed African folk knowledge to do so. In the context of slavery, abortion and infanticide expressed a woman's desperate determination to resist the oppressive conditions of slavery. As [African American feminist and academic] Angela Davis points out, when Black women resorted to abortion, the stories they told were not so much about the desire to be free of pregnancy, but rather about the miserable social conditions that dissuaded them from bringing new lives into the world.

Throughout the nineteenth century, white southerners repeatedly expressed their racist nightmares about a huge Black population increase. In fact, the Black population of the South was growing much more slowly than the white population. In 1870 there were 5 million Blacks in the South, and in 1910 there were 8.7 million, whereas there were 8.6 million whites in 1870 and 20.5 million in 1910.

By the early 1900s Black women were making significant gains in controlling their fertility by marrying late and having few children. In this era the Black women's club movement, the organized voice of African-American women during the late nineteenth and early twentieth centuries, directly addressed issues of Black women's sexuality and sought to "confront and redefine morality and assess its relationship to "true womanhood." Stereotypes about Black women's sexuality and alleged immorality prompted many African-American women to "make the virtues as well as the wants of the colored women known to the American people . . . to put a new social value on themselves." The main organization for Black women's clubs, the National Association of Colored Women, had between 150,000 and 200,000 members, mainly middle-class women, in forty-one states in the mid-1920s. The club movement was integral to the networks that shared contraceptive information and supported "voluntary motherhood."

In 1894 *The Women's Era*, an African-American women's journal edited by Josephine St. Pierre Ruffin, declared that "not all women are intended for mothers. Some of us have not the temperament for family life." Club members and others supported this perspective, and many responded to advertisements in Black newspapers in the early twentieth century for a medicated douche product called Puf, which was reported to "end your calendar worries."

THE BIRTH CONTROL CAMPAIGN, 1915–1950

Today it is commonplace to link the emergence of the birth control movement in the early twentieth century to the coercion of African-American women by a population control establishment anxious to limit Black fertility. While the population control establishment may have had its agenda, African Americans were willingly involved in the national birth control debate for their own reasons. African-American women were sensitive to the intersection of race, gender, and class issues that affected their drive for equality in early-twentieth-century American society. According to historian Jessie Rodrique, grassroots African Americans were "active and effective participants in the establishment of local [family-planning] clinics . . . and despite cooperation with white birth control groups, Blacks maintained a degree of independence" that allowed the development of an African-American analysis of family planning and the role it played in racial progress.

African-American women saw themselves not as breeders or matriarchs but as builders and nurturers of a race, a nation. Sojourner Truth's statement, "I feel as if the power of a nation is within me!" affirmed the role of African-American women as "seminal forces of the endurance and creativity needed by future generations of Blacks not merely to survive, but to thrive, produce, and progress."

In this spirit, the Black women's club movement supported the establishment of family-planning clinics in Black communities. In 1918 the Women's Political Association of Harlem became the first Black organization to schedule lectures on birth control. They were soon joined by dozens of other clubwomen seeking information about birth control in their communities. The National Urban League requested that the Birth Control Federation of America (the forerunner to Planned Parenthood) open a clinic in the Columbus Hill section of the Bronx in 1925. Several ministers held discussions about birth control at their churches, and in 1932 the Reverend Adam Clayton Powell of the Abyssinian Baptist Church spoke at public meetings in support of family planning.

African-American organizations, including the National Association for the Advancement of Colored People (NAACP), the National Urban League, and leading Black newspapers like the *San Francisco Spokesman* (1932) and the *Pittsburgh Courier* (1936) promoted family planning. The Black press espoused this strategy as a means for uplifting the race, perhaps partially in response to the economic ravages of the Depression. The African-American newspapers of the period also reported the mortality rate of women who had septic abortions and championed the causes of Black doctors who were arrested for performing illegal abortions.

The *Baltimore Afro-American* wrote that pencils, nails, and hat pins were instruments commonly used for self-induced abortions, and that abortions among Black women were deliberate, not the spontaneous result of poor health or sexually transmitted diseases. Statistics on abortions among African-American women are scarce, but 28 percent of Black women surveyed by an African-American doctor in Nashville in 1940 said they had had at least one abortion.

REACTION

The opposition to fertility control for women in the 1920s came primarily from the Catholic Church, from white conservatives who feared the availability of birth control for white women, and from Black nationalist leaders like Marcus Garvey, who believed in increasing the African population in response to racial oppression. President Theodore Roosevelt condemned the tendency toward smaller family sizes among white women as race suicide. He denounced family planning as "criminal against the race."

As racism, lynchings, and poverty took their heavy toll on African Americans in the early twentieth century, fears of depopulation arose within a rising Black nationalist movement. These fears produced a pronatalist shift in the views of African Americans. The change from relative indifference about population size to using population growth as a form of political currency presaged the inevitable conflict between those who believed in the right of Black women to exercise bodily self-determination and those who stressed the African-American community's need to foster political and economic self-determination.

In the United States, eugenics proponents believed that the future of native-born whites in America was threatened by the increasing population of people of color and whites who were not of Nordic-Teutonic descent. The eugenics movement not only affected the thinking in social Darwinist scientific circles, but it also grew to affect public policy, receiving the endorsement of President Calvin Coolidge, who said in 1924, "America must be kept American. Biological laws show . . . that Nordics deteriorate when mixed with other races."

Unlike Malthus, the neo-Malthusians of the eugenics movement believed in contraception, at least for those they deemed inferior. To promote the reproduction of self-defined "racially superior" people, eugenics proponents argued for both "positive" methods, such as tax incentives and education for the desirable types, and "negative" methods, such as sterilization, involuntary confinement, and immigration restrictions for the undesirables. The United States became the first nation in the world to permit mass sterilization as part of an effort to "purify the race." By the mid-1930s about 20,000 Americans had been sterilized against their will, and twenty-one states had passed eugenics laws.

Among supporters of eugenics were not only the rabid haters

in the Ku Klux Klan but also respectable mainstream white Americans who were troubled by the effects of urbanization, industrialization, and immigration. During this same period, thousands of Blacks fled the Jim Crow South and migrated to the North. These fast-paced demographic changes alarmed many nativist whites, who questioned birth control for themselves but approved it as a way to contain people of color and immigrants.

When the movement for birth control began, organizers like Margaret Sanger believed that fertility control was linked to upward social mobility for all women, regardless of race or immigrant status. Because the medical establishment largely opposed birth control, Sanger initially emphasized woman-controlled methods that did not depend on medical assistance. Her arguments persuaded middle-class women, both Black and white, to use birth control when available.

Sanger's immediate effect on African-American women was to help transform their covert support for and use of family planning into the visible public support of activists in the club movement. But African-American women envisioned an even more pointed concept of reproductive justice: the freedom to have, or not to have, children.

The early feminism of the birth control movement, which promoted equality and reproductive rights for all women regardless of race or economic status, collapsed under the weight of support offered by the growing number of nativist whites. Under the influence of eugenicists, Sanger changed her approach, as did other feminists. In 1919 her American Birth Control League began to rely heavily for legitimacy on medical doctors and the growing eugenics movement. The eugenics movement provided scientific and authoritative language that legitimated women's right to contraception. This co-optation of the birth control movement produced racist depopulation policies and doctor-controlled birth control technology.

The resulting racist and anti-immigrant public policies assumed Black and immigrant women had a moral obligation to restrict the size of their families. While birth control was demanded as a right and an option for privileged women, it became an obligation for the poor. In 1934 Guy Irving Burch, founder of the Population Reference Bureau, said, "I think there is good reason to be optimistic about the future of the native [white] American stock if birth control is made available to the millions of aliens in our cities and the millions of colored people in this country."

African Americans protested these policies. The *Pittsburgh Courier*, a Black newspaper with an editorial policy that favored family planning, advocated in 1936 that African Americans should oppose depopulation programs proposed by eugenicists because the burden would "fall upon colored people and it behooves us to watch the law and stop the spread" of eugenic sterilization.

One such program was the Negro Project, designed by Sanger's Birth Control Federation in 1939. It hired several African-American ministers to travel through the South to recruit African-American doctors. The project proposal included a quote by W. E. B. DuBois, saying that "the mass of ignorant Negroes still breed carelessly and disastrously, so that the increase among Negroes, even more than the increase among Whites, is from that part of the population least intelligent and fit, and least able to rear their children properly." This quote, often mistakenly attributed to Sanger, reflected the shared race and class biases of the project's founders.

The Negro Project relied on Black ministers because of its white sponsors' belief that "the most successful educational approach to the Negro is through a religious appeal." Sanger wrote, "We do not want word to go out that we want to exterminate the Negro population and the minister is the man who can straighten out that idea if it ever occurs to any of their more rebellious members." The doctors recruited by the ministers were supposed to work for the project for free or, at best, demand payment from their patients. In contrast, the Birth Control Federation at the time paid most of the white doctors who worked on its behalf.

According to historian Linda Gordon, the project was the product of elitist birth control programs, whose design eliminated the possibility of popular, grassroots involvement in promoting birth control as a cause. Notions of civil rights, women's rights, or combating southern poverty were missing from this program. Politicians in southern states at this time were particularly interested in spreading birth control among African Americans to limit Black population growth, which could threaten their political and economic hegemony.

It is extremely likely that the racism of the birth control organizers, coupled with the genocidal assumptions of eugenics supporters, increased Black distrust of the public health system and has fueled Black opposition to family planning up to the present time. By 1949 approximately 2.5 million African-American women were organized in social and political clubs and organizations. Many of them supported birth control and abortion, but at the same time they offered a strong critique of the eugenicists. A clear sense of dual or "paired" values emerged among African-American women: they wanted individual control over their bodies, but at the same time they resisted government and private depopulation policies that blurred the distinction between incentives and coercion.

The Birth Control and Abortion Movements Have a Shared Purpose

MARGARET SANGER

Margaret Sanger was a pivotal figure in the fight for woman's rights in the United States and is often seen as the leading force of the birth control movement in America. She believed that large families were the cause of poverty and thus rallied for birth control and family planning. In 1913 Sanger began publishing the monthly newspaper *Woman Rebel*, which she used to espouse her beliefs about birth control, and which led to her arrest. Sanger's passion did not wane however, and in 1916 she found herself in jail again, this time for opening a clinic. She continued to open clinics across the United States and to encourage women to lobby for their rights. Thirty years after she opened her first clinic, Sanger cofounded International Planned Parenthood, an organization that would ultimately be seen as the most important organization of the abortion movement.

The following selection is from Margaret Sanger's book *Woman and the New Race*. Written in 1920 during the height of the first wave of feminism, Sanger used this book to promote her beliefs on a number of controversial topics including the inequalities between the sexes, overpopulation, poverty, morality, abortion, and birth control. The excerpt that follows is taken from the chapter entitled "Why Not Birth-Control Clinics in America?" In this chapter Sanger draws the connection between birth control clinics and abortion and argues that with widespread availability of birth control in clinics, the danger involved in abortion would be avoided. In effect, she argues that birth

Margaret Sanger, *Woman and the New Race*. New York: Brentano's, 1920.

control is a preventive medicine, which can aid both women and society as a whole.

The absurd cruelty of permitting thousands of women each year to go through abortions to prevent the aggravation of diseases for which they are under treatment assuredly cannot be much longer ignored by the medical profession. Responsibility for the inestimable damage done by the practice of permitting patients suffering from certain ailments to become pregnant, because of their ignorance of contraceptives, when the physician knows that if pregnancy goes to its full term it will hasten the disease and lead to the patient's death, must in all fairness be laid at his door.

What these diseases are and what dangers are involved in pregnancy are known to every practitioner of standing. Specialists have not been negligent in pointing out the situation. Eager to enhance or protect their reputations in the profession, they continually call out to one another: "Don't let the patient bear a child—don't let pregnancy continue."

CONDITIONS FOR ABORTION

The warning has been sounded most often, perhaps, in the cases of tubercular women. "In view of the fact that the tubercular process becomes exacerbated either during pregnancy or after childbirth, most authorities recommend that abortion be induced as a matter of routine in all tubercular women," says Dr. J. Whitridge Williams, obstetrician-in-chief to the Johns Hopkins Hospital, in his treatise on *Obstetrics.* Dr. Thomas Watts Eden, obstetrician and gynecologist to Charing Cross Hospital and member of the staffs of other notable British hospitals, extends but does not complete the list in this paragraph on page 652 of his *Practical Obstetrics:* "Certain of the conditions enumerated form absolute indications for the induction of abortion. These are nephritis, uncompensated valvular lesions of the heart, advanced tuberculosis, insanity, irremediable malignant tumors, hydatidiform mole, uncontrollable uterine hemorrhage, and acute hydramnios."

POTENTIAL DANGERS EASILY AVOIDED

We know that abortion, when performed by skilled hands, under right conditions, brings almost no danger to the life of the patient, and we also know that particular diseases can be more

Leader of the birth control movement, Margaret Sanger, waits to testify before a Senate subcommittee on whether physicians should make birth control available to their patients.

easily combatted after such an abortion than during a pregnancy allowed to come to full term. But why not adopt the easier, safer, less repulsive course and prevent conception altogether? Why put these thousands of women who each year undergo such abortions to the pain they entail and in whatever danger attends them?

Why continue to send home women to whom pregnancy is a grave danger with the futile advice: "Now don't get this way again!" They are sent back to husbands who have generations of passion and passion's claim to outlet. They are sent back without being given information as to how to prevent the dangerous pregnancy and are expected, presumably, to depend for their safety upon the husband's continence. The wife and husband are thrown together to bring about once more the same condition. Back comes the patient again in a few months to be aborted and told once more not to do it again.

Does any physician believe that the picture is overdrawn? I have known of many such cases. A recent one that came under my observation was that of a woman who suffered from a disease of the kidneys. Five times she was taken to a maternity hospital in an ambulance after falling in offices or in the street. One of the foremost gynecologists of America sent her out three times without giving her information as to the contraceptive means which would have prevented a repetition of this experience.

Why does this situation exist? We do not question the good intent nor the high purposes of these physicians. We know that they observe a high standard of ethics and that they are working for the uplift of the race. But here is a situation that is absurd—hideously absurd. What is the matter?

Several factors contribute to this state of affairs. First, the subject of contraception has been kept in the dark, even in medical colleges and in hospitals. Abortion has been openly discussed as a necessity under certain conditions, but the subject of contraception, as any physician will admit, has not yet been brought to the front. It has escaped specialized attention in the laboratories and the research departments. Thus there has been no professional stamp of approval by great bodies of experimenters. The result is that the average physician has felt that contraceptive methods are not yet established as certainties and has, for that reason, refused to direct *their use.*

THE SOLUTION

Specialists are so busy with their own particular subjects and general practitioners are so taken up with their daily routine that they cannot give to the problem of contraception the attention it must have. Consultation rooms in charge of reputable physicians who have specialized in contraception, assisted by registered nurses—in a word, clinics designed for this specialty, would meet this crying need. Such clinics should deal with each woman individually, taking into account her particular disease, her temperament, her mentality and her condition, both physical and economic. Their sole function should be to prevent pregnancy. In accomplishing this purpose, a higher standard of hygiene is attained. Not only would a burden be removed from the physician who sends a woman to such a clinic, but there would be an improvement in the woman's general condition which would in a number of ways reflect itself in benefit to her family.

BIRTH CONTROL AS PREVENTIVE MEDICINE

All this for the diseased woman. But every argument that can be made for preventive medicine can be made for birth-control clinics for the use of the woman who has not yet lost her health. Sound and vigorous at the time of her marriage, she could remain so if given advice as to by what means she could space her children and limit their number. When she is not given such information, she is plunged blindly into married life and a few years is likely to find her with a large family, herself diseased and damaged, an unfit breeder of the unfit, and still ignorant!

What are the fruits of this woeful ignorance in which women have been kept? First, a tremendous infant mortality— hundreds of thousands of babies dying annually of diseases which flourish in poverty and neglect.

Next, the rapid increase of the feebleminded, of criminal types and of the pathetic victims of toil in the child-labor factories. Another result is the familiar overcrowding of tenements, the forcing of the children into the street, the ensuing prostitution, alcoholism and almost universal physical and moral unfitness.

Those abhorrent conditions point to a blunder upon the part of those to whom we have entrusted the care of the health of the individual, the family and the race. The medical profession, neglecting the principle involved in preventive medicine, has permitted these conditions to come about.

Increased Birth Control May Not Diminish Demand for Abortion

MARY STEICHEN CALDERONE

The following excerpt is taken from the transcript of a conference sponsored by the Planned Parenthood Federation of America in 1955, the proceedings of which were attended and edited by physician Mary Steichen Calderone. Calderone was the medical director of the Planned Parenthood Federation of America from 1953 to 1965. Arguably her greatest achievement as director was in 1964 when the American Medical Association broke from their traditionally repressive stance on abortion and agreed that it was the responsibility of the medical profession to give out information on all aspects of reproduction. She went on to cofound and become executive director of the Sex Information and Education Council of the United States (SIECUS), an organization established to research, discuss, and educate Americans on the topic of human sexuality.

In this transcript a number of medical doctors from across the United States attempt to identify whether accessible birth control would diminish the need for abortions. One pivotal position presented at the conference was that if birth control was readily available and accessible, the demand for abortion should decrease. However, another position examined the idea that even when contraceptives are made available, unwanted pregnancies might still occur. In due course the doctors could not come to a definitive answer, but they did come to the conclusion that there was a relationship between birth control and abortion.

Mary Steichen Calderone, *Abortion in the United States: A Conference Sponsored by the Planned Parenthood Federation of America, Inc.* New York: Harper and Brothers, 1958. Copyright © 1958 by Paul B. Hoeber, Inc. Renewed in 1986 by Harper & Row Publishers, Inc. All rights reserved. Reproduced by permission of Lippincott, Williams & Wilkins.

C HAIRMAN DOUGLASS: In this session we will discuss what relationship, if any, exists between availability of contraceptive services and the incidence of illegal abortion—or to put it another way, we will try to find out if the one acts as a deterrent to the other.

DR. SHANHOLTZ: I have heard the statement made that abortions, illegal or therapeutic, might be considered a sort of measure of failure in connection with Planned Parenthood efforts. Of course, being a public health man, I think entirely in terms of prevention. So if we could get the idea of *planning* to work, if every pregnancy were planned, then the demand for abortions presumably would decrease in proportion. There might still be some demand, because parents might change their minds about wanting the child after conception, or there might, after pregnancy had begun, be discovered some disease that would be a reason for therapeutic interruption. A third reason might be failure of the contraceptive method. These three categories might account for some small demand for abortions, even if contraception were widely available.

I cannot speak for other states, but down in Virginia we are doing something about family planning. The state sponsors about one hundred eighty general maternity clinics. And each one, almost without exception, does offer post-partum advice on contraception to those deemed by the physician in charge to be eligible for and in need of it. There are certain areas where there is a considerable percentage of Catholics, and maybe even a health officer or a clinician who is a Catholic, but the majority of the clinics do offer contraceptive advice. This program in Virginia is the result of co-operation on the part of the State House and the Planned Parenthood League of Virginia.

There is another thing about these clinics that is worth mentioning: I gather from Dr. Kinsey and from Dr. Kleegman that this type of advice is least available to the less well-educated, lower-income groups, and those are mainly the groups that our clinics serve. For instance, we get many cases referred in by midwives or by private physicians for the reason that they are not financially able to seek such help from their own family physician.

DR. CALDERONE: A professor of obstetrics once remarked to me that he hated doing therapeutic abortions in spite of their being medically indicated, and whenever such a case was referred to him from another service, he considered that the referring service had failed grossly in the practice of preventive medicine, by not having referred the patient for contraception to prevent her ever needing an abortion. . . .

DR. KINSEY: I should like to make a remark about the situations under which unwanted pregnancies occur. We have spent considerable time inquiring into the matter. You cannot define any correlation between the contraceptive practice of a particular couple and the occurrence of unwanted pregnancies with that couple, because in 99 per cent of the time they will use an effective contraceptive, but the physiology and the psychology of sexual response is such that there do come situations when they are aroused and completely forget the desirability of using precautionary methods, or they happen to be away from home and it is inconvenient to secure the means of practicing the methods. Thus a certain portion of unwanted pregnancies *in marriage* come out of just such situations, and with these it is not a case of lack of contraceptive knowledge, but a case of the impossibility of completely changing the psychology and physiology of the human animal to lead it to react like a machine 100 per cent of the time.

In regard to the unwanted pregnancies that come outside of marriage, in our experience these more often occur among the religiously devout who set out on a date with the determination that they are not going to be sinful and have coitus and, with such a conviction in mind, will of course not carry contraceptives. They end up doing so, and thus we see in some of the most devout two, three, and four extramarital pregnancies, leading ultimately to abortion or to forced marriage.

I have this further remark concerning effective contraceptive measures. We have questioned all our subjects as to the acceptability of the ones presently available. There is widespread dislike of the methods in general use.

Consequently, if any group interested in family planning

wants to help reduce the number of unwanted pregnancies by the use of contraceptives, they are going to have to develop a more easily used and more acceptable contraceptive than is ordinarily available today.

DR. CALDERONE: I am very much interested in the contribution of the public health people here, and it seems to me that they have brought a rather new element into this whole picture. We are talking about abortion, and they have been talking about contraceptive services within their states. Have we established the premise that contraception per se actually could be a favorable factor in the prevention of abortion? It is not clear in my mind that this connection has been established.

DR. MCLANE: I will stand by the statement that if there were a satisfactory and effective contraceptive, and if everyone used it every time they had intercourse, there would be no abortions. But we haven't yet gotten to that point. There are too many "ifs."

DR. KINSEY: At the risk of being repetitious, I would remind the group that we have found the highest frequency of induced abortion in the group which, in general, most frequently uses contraceptives.

I don't think it is entirely carelessness. As I pointed out before, you don't do anything—putting on your clothes, or going to bed, or drinking, or eating—with absolute regularity. And I think it is just too much to hope that we can ever have any contraceptive practice, outside of temporary sterilization, which is going to prevent this occasional slip that accounts for a high proportion of undesired pregnancies and abortions, especially among those of the upper socioeconomic levels.

DR. SHANHOLTZ: How do you account for the fact that the size of families is so much larger in the less-educated, lower-income group than in the higher-educated group?

DR. KINSEY: The pregnancy rate is definitely higher, the use of contraceptives is lower, and the abortion rate is lower. All these factors add up to the higher birth rate in the lower-income group.

DR. WHELPTON: If you deal with those persons who are successful in planning family size in this country and in some other parts of the world, you find the opposite relation: The higher the income, the larger the number of children, *when children are planned*. In other words, the customary widespread inverse relation between income and family size is due mainly to the differences in the proportion of persons using contraception or using it effectively in the different income classes.

While I would not disagree with Dr. Kinsey that, among those who really want to control families, you find a high proportion using contraception, as well as an important number of abortions, it seems to me that there is another way of looking at this question.

If you can increase the proportion of persons who use contraception to control family size, or if you can give persons who want to control family size but have not previously been able to do it a means of doing so by contraception instead of by abortion, it is quite possible that you can get a substantial decrease in the intentional abortion rate.

DR. KOLB: I would like to support Dr. Kinsey's remarks that contraceptives, no matter how effective, are unlikely to eliminate abortion completely. When you have the opportunity of following groups of people, in studying their attitudes at the time they conceive and later on, you become aware of the fact that the biological urge can overwhelm them, no matter what intellectual insight they might have into the use of contraceptives; and then, at a later date, their rational attitudes may dictate to them the idea of abortion.

DR. GALDSTON: I think we ought to go back and have a definite answer to Dr. Calderone's question. I would like to offer here a negative one, for the simple reason that I do not believe a positive one is possible.

I think unless one reduces to the level of the nonsensical the correlation between contraception and abortion, assuming on the one hand that of course, if you didn't have any contraception, you would have many more abortions and, on the other hand, as Dr. McLane presupposes, that perfect and universal contraception would eliminate any need for illegal abortions, one cannot really arrive at any definite answer on the problem of relation of contraception to abortion.

The fact of the matter is that a two-factor relationship—between contraception and unwanted pregnancy—is too gross an oversimplification of a very involved complex of interrelated factors.

I want to support what Dr. Kolb said from experiences in psychiatry. Not uncommonly a young lady who has been going around with a young man in her judgment all too long, might think that, if she becomes pregnant, it would hasten the marriage. Sometimes it does and sometimes it does not.

Again, a woman who is utterly frustrated in her relationship with a man may try to compensate for her frustrations by becoming pregnant, only to find that the unsatisfactory relationship is aggravated rather than made tolerable by the pregnancy.

I think therefore the only way that we can answer the question Dr. Calderone raised is by saying that there is no direct *proportionate* relationship between contraception and abortion.

DR. STONE: I should like to take issue with my good friend Dr. Galdston. I believe that there *is* a high correlation between the lack of use of contraception and the high incidence of abortion: the more contraception is used, the less abortion there will be.

While I do not have the figures here, I know from the more than 140,000 couples that have come to the Margaret Sanger Research Bureau that those who have come early in marriage and obtained competent contraceptive information have had definitely fewer abortions than those who have not used any contraceptive measures at all.

DR. GALDSTON: I didn't say there wasn't any relationship. What I said was that there was not a *direct* relationship; in other words, 100 per cent information will not lead you to a 100 per cent result.

DR. LIDZ: Although I agree with Dr. Kolb and Dr. Galdston and also with Dr. Stone, I think we have been talking almost as though the question is that all unwanted pregnancies are going to be aborted. Now, families may be practicing contraception and, naturally, there are going to be both accidental slips in technique and unconscious slips for more or less purposeful reasons, but I think that usually married couples in the younger age groups will go along with even an unplanned-for pregnancy. Nevertheless I would be very much surprised if we didn't find that a pretty strong relationship does exist between the use of contraception and fewer abortions.

After all, if no contraception were used, even the upper economic classes would be having seven, eight and nine pregnancies, and there would certainly be a higher abortion rate. . . .

DR. CALDERONE: I believe Dr. Kinsey brought out that most of the failures were not failures in contraceptive method but failure to use the method, either through ignorance, inertia, or carelessness.

DR. SENIOR: That is still another aspect, yes; but I believe we have to contribute toward a change of climate in society that adds to a person's feeling of personal responsibility; and education has much to do with that.

There are large numbers of persons who take a very fatalistic attitude toward life, who do what they want to do at the moment and think about the consequences afterward. There are educational approaches to this problem too. I think there are probably a number of women . . . who resort to abortion because they have no faith in so-called newfangled ideas. "Newfangled ideas" means contraceptives. Abortion is the method their grandmothers used, so that is going to be the method they also will use to control family size, unless educated to believe and do otherwise. . . .

So that even though we certainly cannot say—and I think this is what Dr. Kinsey and Dr. Galdston were reacting against— that the universal use or even availability of contraceptives is going to solve the problem of abortion, I don't believe we can afford to take the stand that this *is not* going to contribute in some way toward a solution.

CHAPTER 2

THE MOVEMENT FIGHTS TO PRESERVE ABORTION

AMERICAN
SOCIAL
MOVEMENTS

The Women's Movement Adopts the Abortion Issue

SUZANNE STAGGENBORG

The following selection is taken from Suzanne Staggenborg's book *The Pro-Choice Movement: Organization and Activism in the Abortion Conflict*. In it Staggenborg draws historical connections between the women's movement and the abortion movement in America. Staggenborg primarily focuses on the years immediately prior to the legalization of abortion in 1973, and she argues that many woman's rights organizations, including the National Association for the Repeal of Abortion Laws (NARAL) and the National Organization for Women (NOW), were central to the pro-choice movement's endurance and success during its early years. She examines the feminist movement's direct-action tactics and the effectiveness of these methods in forwarding the abortion movement. Staggenborg argues that although the pivotal victory in the abortion rights movement occurred in the legal battle *Roe v. Wade*, huge steps were made when feminists joined the movement. Feminist activism helped create a new social consciousness about the connection between woman's rights and abortion and, through protests and acts of civil disobedience, ensured it was an issue the American public could no longer ignore.

By 1970, the women's liberation movement was a national phenomenon. Feminists were attracting media and public attention by staging demonstrations and raising controversial demands. Abortion was a central feminist issue that was dramatized through direct action: In New York in 1969 the feminist Redstockings held "counter-hearings" to protest the biased state legislative hearings on abortion reform. In Detroit in 1970 a "funeral march" was held by women's liberation activists to protest the deaths of women killed by back-alley abortionists while the legislature debated abortion reform. In Chicago, feminists disrupted the convention of the American Medical Association to protest the AMA's lack of support for abortion law repeal. Throughout the country, feminists staged street theater, "speakouts," and other demonstrations for abortion rights.

For all of its conventional pressure-group tactics, the movement to legalize abortion was very much a part of the protest cycle of the 1960s. Direct-action tactics such as demonstrations had become part of the repertoire of movement participants, and the grass-roots constituents of the population and women's movements could be mobilized to participate in such tactics. The opportunities for direct action and the strong obstacles to achieving legalized abortion through institutionalized channels alone ensured that no movement organization limited its activities solely to institutionalized arenas.

Use of the direct-action tactics of "outside" challengers was facilitated in part by the same organizational characteristics that limited the movement's capacity for influence through established channels. Although formalized organizational structures help movement organizations operate in the world of conventional pressure-group politics, such structures make it more difficult to take quick action and to bypass disputes over radical positions and confrontational tactics. The movement's informal organization in the years before the legalization of abortion allowed movement organizations to take advantage of opportunities for confrontation and direct action, which often involved an element of risk. This was possible in single-issue movement organizations like NARAL [the National Association for the Repeal of Abortion Laws], where a small number of leaders maintained centralized control, and in women's liberation groups like the CWLU [Chicago Women's Liberation Union], which had decentralized structures in which subunits were able to act autonomously. . . .

To understand fully the movement's strategies and tactics in these years, it is necessary to go beyond a strictly organizational analysis to an examination of the feminist approach to abortion, which was an important part of the movement. Women's liberation groups saw themselves as part of a larger movement that was challenging basic social, economic, and political institutions. Their goal was to create participatory democratic institutions that would serve human needs rather than corporate interests. The women's health movement that developed within the younger branch of the women's movement wanted to create a nonprofit, high-quality health care delivery system and to challenge the hierarchical doctor-client relationship, demanding that women participate in their own health care. It was in this larger context that the women's liberation movement addressed the abortion issue. . . .

FEMINIST MOBILIZATION AND DIRECT ACTION

Given the limited support for abortion law repeal from established organizations, the presence of the women's movement was by far the most positive feature of the political environment of the abortion movement in the years following NARAL's founding in 1969. The women's movement was growing rapidly, and the news media were interested in both the abortion issue and the women's movement. In addition to tactics like referral services that were aimed at women, feminists initiated direct-action tactics such as demonstrations that were targeted at established power holders. They also provided support for direct-action tactics initiated by single-issue abortion movement organizations.

Demonstrations by women's movement activists sent a message of public support for abortion rights to established organizations and authorities and served an expressive function for participants. Organizations like the Chicago Women's Liberation Union organized a number of demonstrations that were targeted at representatives of the "establishment," such as the American Medical Association, as well as government officials. In 1970, for example, CWLU activists participated in a demonstration at the convention site of the AMA, and WITCH [radical feminist organization Women's International Terrorist Conspiracy from Hell] activists, who were loosely connected to the CWLU, infiltrated the AMA convention to present a list of demands, including the demand for free legal abortion. When the AMA failed to respond, the WITCHes "hexed" the organization on the following day, and according to a CWLU report "the feeling of exhilaration and sisterhood was so rewarding that the WITCHes decided to hex the business establishment on a regular basis."

Women's movement activists were also critical to the strategies and tactics of a number of other organizations. Because of the visibility of the women's movement, NARAL leaders like Lawrence Lader became firmly convinced that the tiny abortion movement could succeed only by making confrontational demands and engaging in tactics that would attract young feminists as "troops" for the cause, stirring up sympathetic public opinion through the ensuing publicity.

NARAL

NARAL frequently did take advantage of the availability of feminist groups to organize demonstrations. As a result of close ties between NOW [the National Organization for Women] and NARAL, NOW helped launch NARAL through strong participation in NARAL's first national action, a day of "Children by Choice" demonstrations held in conjunction with press conferences in eleven cities on Mother's Day in 1969. Because NOW was growing rapidly in terms of members and chapters in the early 1970s, NOW was able to participate on a number of occasions in demonstrations for abortion law repeal in cooperation with NARAL. Chicago NOW joined other NOW chapters and local women's liberation groups in organizing or participating in demonstrations for abortion law repeal and related issues.

The adoption of confrontational demands and tactics by NARAL in response to the feminist presence in the movement was not inevitable, however. The conference at which NARAL was officially formed brought together abortion activists from across the country who represented a variety of approaches to

changing the abortion laws. Many of the activists were feminists but there were also persons favoring a slower strategy of
working for reform rather than repeal of the laws. Consequently, NARAL activists did not unanimously support the
adoption of confrontational demands and tactics. The decision
to publicly offer legal and financial support for referral services,
for example, was a particularly controversial one in NARAL.
Some NARAL leaders, including Lonny Myers, were concerned that its open connection to referral services left NARAL
open to attack by opponents, and others were concerned about
the financial obligations that might be incurred by activists providing referrals.

NARAL's adoption of radical demands and controversial tactics was due to internal organizational factors in addition to the
influence of the women's movement. With regard to the organizational resources needed to advocate such positions,
Lawrence Lader and other key leaders had experience in providing abortion referrals and knew the legal risks and public relations benefits of doing so. Moreover, Lader had published an
article reporting on the results of his study of women who had
received nonhospital abortions as a result of referrals from abortion movement activists. According to Lader, the article gave the
movement "documentary evidence of the high medical standards of in-office abortion" necessary for its position on freestanding clinics.

Most importantly, NARAL's organizational structure allowed
those leaders of NARAL who advocated confrontational positions to push their strategies. NARAL was centrally controlled
by its executive committee in the pre-1973 period, and its operating procedures were informal. There was no system of ro-
tating individuals off the executive committee every few years,
thereby allowing the "militants" who had a majority on the executive committee, to control the nominating committee. The
NARAL board of directors, which was representative of a
broader range of the NARAL constituency, may have chosen a
more cautious approach, but it was an unwieldy body of up to
ninety members that met only once a year and therefore did not

control the real decision making in the organization. When those leaders on the NARAL executive committee who favored radical demands and confrontational tactics wanted to take action (e.g., call a press conference or a demonstration), they simply picked up the phone to obtain approval from a majority of the executive committee. In this way, action could be taken which bypassed bureaucratic procedures that might have limited NARAL to the adoption of less confrontational tactics. For these reasons, the informal, centralized NARAL organization facilitated the use of tactics favored by the "militants" in the leadership. For example, when leaders like Lader who openly provided referrals for abortions were indicted by a grand jury, they quickly pushed NARAL to provide support.

ZERO POPULATION GROWTH

The strategies of another major organization in the pre-1973 abortion repeal movement, Zero Population Growth [ZPG], were similarly influenced by the growth of the women's movement in the late 1960s and the early 1970s and by internal organizational characteristics. Like NARAL and NOW, ZPG adopted the demand for repeal, rather than reform, of abortion laws, advocating legal abortion as a component of the "basic human right to limit one's own reproduction." ZPG's primary concern, of course, has always been overpopulation, and abortion was advocated, along with contraception and sterilization, as a "means of birth control" that would help bring down the birthrate. Sensitive to the concerns of feminists about its potential coercion of women, however, ZPG conspicuously stressed the voluntary nature of its demands for abortion, sterilization, and contraception and, from the start, expressed its support for women's rights.

ZPG took a "women's rights" approach to abortion in part as a result of overlaps in the national leadership of ZPG and groups like NARAL and NOW. The organization was also influenced by its numerous chapters, many of which consisted of students who were strongly interested in abortion and women's rights. In the early years in Chicago, for example, a number of campus-based ZPG chapters were working for repeal alongside feminists. Although there was also a more conservative element in ZPG's local constituency, the organization's decision-making structure allowed national leaders, who tended to be sympathetic to women's rights, to maintain control over ZPG's positions.

In general, the presence of the women's movement was a strong influence on the strategic and tactical choices of the abortion movement. Not only did women's movement organizations initiate many direct-action tactics, but various other kinds of organizations also sought to use both the energies of feminists and the repertoire of tactics associated with the women's movement and other movements of the 1960s. NARAL frequently mobilized feminist support for its actions. And in 1971 many feminist groups contributed to the success of the nationwide demonstrations organized by the SWP-backed Women's National Abortion Action Coalition (WONAAC), which received significant media coverage. . . .

CONCLUSION

Before 1973, the confrontational direct-action tactics of political "outsiders" were as much a part of the movement to legalize abortion as were the conventional means of influence used by seasoned activists. The presence of the women's movement in the expanded social movement sector of the 1960s was an important factor prompting the use of these tactics. Feminists took to the streets to demand abortion rights, but they also worked to create a new social consciousness about women's rights to abortion. Although direct-action tactics did not have the direct impact that litigation had on the legalization of abortion, they helped bring the abortion issue to public attention and created an atmosphere of support for legal abortion. Moreover, the alternative institutions and cultural changes created by the women's health movement would have an important influence on subsequent collective action.

Feminist Health Agencies Fight for Safe and Legal Access to Abortion

KATHLEEN C. BERKELEY

Kathleen C. Berkeley is a professor of history at the University of North Carolina, Wilmington, and the author of *The Women's Liberation Movement in America*, from which the following extract is taken. Berkeley explores the way in which the emergence of the women's liberation movement and the concept of feminism affected the abortion rights movement. She contends that the introduction of feminism and the emphasis on women's control over their own bodies resulted in the establishment of women's health centers and clinics, which would prove to be instrumental in the abortion rights movement. Feminist health advocates questioned the methods of the patriarchal medical profession, who had controlled the practice and ultimately the repressive public perception of abortion in America for decades. Women's physical, mental, and emotional well-being became a central issue.

T he right to control one's body was at the heart of the feminist health movement and was interpreted by feminists to mean possessing knowledge about how their bodies functioned, having the power to make informed decisions about their bodies, and being treated with dignity and respect by the medical establishment. Education and self-help were key components of the early phase of the feminist health movement, but soon feminist concerns about the relationship between sexuality and reproduction would require activists to lobby for concrete changes in medical practices and the passage of new public policy initiatives.

The 1970 publication of *Women and Their Bodies* (soon to be retitled *Our Bodies, Ourselves*) gave the women's health movement its proverbial shot in the arm. This project, conceived and written by a small, radical feminist collective from Boston, grew out of a women's liberation conference held in the city during the spring of 1969. Following the success of the conference, a dozen women conducted a free course on women's health issues for individuals and community groups; so popular was this course that the women, who eventually incorporated themselves as the *Boston Women's Health Book Collective*, decided to publish their research on women's health issues. The book became a runaway best-seller with over 200,000 copies sold by 1973 and over 2 million by the end of the decade. Much of the book's focus, like the women's health movement in general, centered on such topics as sexuality (heterosexuality and homosexuality), reproduction (from menstruation to menopause), abortion, violence against women, and lessons in self-defense. The authors' growing awareness of the politics of health care also led them to include a critique of the American health-care system.

Boston feminists were not alone in their determination to educate women about their bodies. In Los Angeles a consciousness-raising group moved from talk to action in the early 1970s. At first, the group limited itself to providing free pregnancy tests and instructions in self-examination (for the treatment of common yeast infections and early detection of venereal diseases). Soon, however, the women added an abortion referral service (abortions were legal in California after 1967, but services were restrictive and expensive), and by 1973, a full-fledged, female-operated clinic offered a full range of gynecological services.

WOMEN'S HEALTH CENTERS

Within a few years the concept of founding women's health centers/clinics had caught fire; and by mid-decade there were over forty such institutions in operation around the United States (the movement also had spread to Canada and Great Britain). Although the feminist health movement remained community-oriented, the mid-1970s witnessed the start of a series of national conferences (the first of which was held at Harvard Medical School and was organized by the *Boston Women's Health Book Collective*) and the formation of the National Women's Health Network. African Americans, Hispanics, and Native Americans joined the mainstream women's health movement, but they also created separate, spin-off organizations that focused specifically on women's health problems that, they argued, were exacerbated by racism (teen pregnancy, high infant-mortality rates, forced sterilization, fetal alcohol syndrome, and pesticide-related infections and diseases). In 1981 Byllye Avery began the National Black Women's Health Project; in 1986 Luz Alvarez Martinez started the National Latina Health Organization; and in 1988 Charon Asetoyer opened the Native American Women's Health and Education Resource Center.

Feminist health advocates frequently tangled with the male-dominated medical establishment. They questioned the wisdom of doctors who prescribed antidepressant drugs or recommended hysterectomies as routine "cures" for women's ailments (both physical and mental), and they parted company with those in the profession who insisted that pregnancy was a disease that needed treatment. Feminists were especially insistent that physicians inform them about the changes taking place in their bodies (during pregnancy) and in fetal development so that they could make informed decisions about the birthing process. They also advocated for the introduction of "natural childbirth" techniques by pushing hospitals to open labor and delivery rooms to coaches (usually, but not always the father) and by refusing drugs that rendered them unconscious (and therefore passive) during childbirth. Finally, feminist health advocates insisted that women had the right to control their fertility and to enjoy their sexuality without suffering the consequences of an unplanned pregnancy. This assertion led to the demand for safe and effective methods of birth control and for unrestricted access to abortion procedures.

THE LEGALITY AND ACCESIBILITY OF ABORTION

Abortion had never been completely outlawed in the United States; instead, for almost a century, this medical procedure was controlled by the state and the medical community. In the years following World War II, this alliance had grown increasingly uneasy from the perspective of the medical profession's more liberal members, many of whom were beginning to question the state's "right" to intervene in a doctor's professional decision. At issue was the definition of acceptable (meaning legal and medical) guidelines for performing a "therapeutic" abortion. The long-accepted legal position held that "therapeutic abortions were performed for physical indications only [after] a thorough hospital review procedure and only in hospitals." By the 1950s, some physicians were applying a more liberal interpetation to the law and were willing to accept "social, economic, and psychiatric indications for therapeutic abortions."

Doctors desirous of securing legal protection for a broader interpretation of the penal code welcomed Planned Parenthood Federation of America's role in organizing a 1955 conference to discuss reforming abortion laws. By the late 1950s, the liberal wing of the legal profession, represented by the American Law Institute, appeared ready to join with the reform wing of the medical profession. In 1959 the American Law Institute took the bold step of drafting a "model abortion law" that would allow "licensed physicians to perform abortions for physical and mental health reasons, fetal defects, or when pregnancy was the result of rape or incest." On the eve of feminism's reemergence as a potent political force, abortion reform advocates remained more concerned with protecting the rights of doctors (including the right to be free from prosecution) than they were with protecting the rights of pregnant women. Still, the model law's existence was a positive and progressive step; over the next several years state medical and legal organizations used the model law to lobby for changes in their local legislatures.

Once feminists joined the debate over abortion, women's physical and mental health and the well-being of the fetus took center stage. Therapeutic abortions had always existed as an option, and in the wake of two tragic and well-publicized incidents in the early 1960s, grounds for performing them slowly became more liberal (between 1962 and 1964 the nation was made aware of the dangers of thalidomide, a tranquilizer routinely prescribed for pregnant women, which caused hideous birth defects, and the serious threat posed to fetal development when women in the early stages of pregnancy were exposed to rubella or "German measles"). Still, this costly procedure remained under the control of the male-dominated medical community. Thus, whereas many (but certainly not all) middle- and upper-class married women were able to secure a therapeutic abortion, poor women, unmarried women, and women in rural areas were never as fortunate. As feminists pointed out, a woman's inability to obtain a safe, legal abortion did not always act as a deterrent. Instead many women (from all classes, races, and ethnic groups) took their chances with illegal abortions; many women suffered severe complications from these illegal procedures, and many women died. By the early 1960s, the medical staff of Chicago's Cook County Hospital, "reported caring annually for nearly five thousand women with abortion related complications." A decade earlier, Los Angeles County Hospital reported two thousand cases per year, and hospital records in New York City indicated that between 1951 and 1962 "the absolute number of abortion deaths nearly doubled from twenty-seven in the early 1950s to fifty-one per year in the early 1960s."

MOBILIZATION TO REPEAL ABORTION LAWS

A few forward-thinking groups took up the issue of abortion repeal prior to NOW [the National Organization for Women] entering the debate. In 1961 the California-based Society for Humane Abortion began by lobbying the state legislature to repeal its antiabortion measure. Within a few years, the group moved from lobbying to direct action by operating an abortion referral service (women were directed to clinics where safe but illegal abortions were performed). By the mid- to late 1960s, such covert "counseling" services, like the one begun by Chicago feminists operating under the name of "Jane," existed in several of the country's large urban areas.

These and other acts of civil disobedience, ... helped to redefine the terms of the abortion debate. Abortion referral providers viewed their actions as political statements, not criminal acts; speak-outs were public events designed to remove the feelings of shame, humiliation, and illegitimacy associated with abortion. Thus, abortion became a legitimate political issue for the public to debate and to resolve through the political process.

Between 1967 and 1971 the repeal wing of the abortion movement gained momentum. In 1967 California, Colorado, and North Carolina became the "first" states in the nation to pass abortion reform legislation. By the end of the decade, twelve more states had passed similar measures, and reform adovocates were confident that more states would follow this trend toward liberalization. In 1969 a national conference on abortion in Chicago produced a new lobbying organization, the National Association for the Repeal of Abortion Laws (Betty Friedan represented NOW at National Association for the Repeal of Abortion Laws inaugural meeting), and a Harris Poll found that almost two-thirds of those interviewed agreed that abortion was a private matter.

VICTORY?

In 1971 the Supreme Court entered the debate over abortion by agreeing to hear two cases, one that examined the constitutionality of a restrictive, nineteenth century abortion law—the *Roe v. Wade* case from Texas—and the other that challenged the constitutionality of the more recent abortion reform legislation—the *Doe v. Bolton* case from Georgia. Almost eighteen months later, on January 22, 1973, the Court issued its historic ruling, but one that fell short of unqualified support for the feminist position, which sought constitutional guarantees for abortion under the equal protection clause as well as under the right to privacy. . . .

With these two decisions, abortion became a legal medical

procedure. It also became a decision that women were entitled to make with some degree of constitutional protection; and for that reason, feminists celebrated the Supreme Court's companion rulings. According to numerous scholars, however, the *Roe* and *Doe* decisions "broke no new constitutional ground; but instead, left the door open for statutory restrictions on abortion even though the medical procedure was declared legal." The surprise for feminists would be the speed with which the opposition would march through that door.

An Abortion Activist Tells Her Story

LESLIE J. REAGAN

In the following article writer, historian, feminist, and activist Leslie J. Reagan profiles the life of Patricia Maginnis, renegade abortion rights activist and founder of the Association for the Repeal of Abortion Laws (ARAL). Reagan uses Maginnis's life to explore the tactics used by abortion rights organizations during the years that abortion was illegal in the United States. According to Reagan, by creating, maintaining, and distributing a list of Mexican abortion providers, Maginnis created an alternative feminist health system, a system that challenged the patriarchal nature of law and medicine. She held ARAL classes where she taught female anatomy, reproduction, and contraception. In the class "the list" was made available to any woman in need, but recognizing that circumstances existed which made going to Mexico impossible, Maginnis also taught women how to self-induce abortions, although she discouraged this method. Through educating women and encouraging them to join the movement and help other women in the same situation, Maginnis created a humane environment whereby women could support each other and were able to control their own reproductive health.

At a time when the topic of abortion was nearly completely surpressed in the public arena, [activist Patricia] Maginnis moved discussion of abortion law reform from professional meetings to the streets. In 1961, Assemblyman John T. Knox presented the first reform bill in California to permit therapeutic abortions for a broader range of reasons, including rape, incest, and congenital fetal defects. Maginnis initiated a petition supporting the bill and collected a thousand signatures. She and

Leslie J. Reagan, "Crossing the Border for Abortions: California Activists, Mexican Clinics, and the Creation of a Feminist Health Agency in the 1960s," *Feminist Studies,* vol. 26, Summer 2000. Copyright © 2000 by Feminist Studies, Inc. Reproduced by permission.

her partner, Robert Bick, also surveyed a cross-section of the San Jose population and discovered the general public's underlying support for "good medical care for abortion." Despite her legwork on behalf of the Knox bill, Maginnis soon repudiated reform laws because of their restrictiveness. She appraised proposed legal reforms from the perspective of women who needed abortions, particularly women who were not wealthy; in this, she was unique in the early 1960s. She became the first to demand complete repeal of the nation's criminal abortion laws. In 1962 she founded the Citizens' Committee for Humane Abortion Laws (later renamed the Society for Humane Abortion), which advocated repeal. Maginnis's activism developed within a larger countercultural political milieu and radical health movement in the San Francisco Bay Area, but she was singular in her untiring commitment to legal abortion for women. By 1965, SHA had 200 members, two of whom—Rowena Gurner and Lana Clarke Phelan—joined Maginnis in devoting themselves to the cause.

THE VOLUNTEERS

The leaders of this California effort were white working women, who had all had illegal abortions. Their backgrounds remind us that Second Wave feminism arose from the working class as well as the middle class. Patricia Maginnis was from a large, not very well off Catholic family from Oklahoma, attended San Jose State College on the GI bill, and supported herself as a laboratory technician. Indeed, Maginnis's manner and look were the opposite of the privileged woman, although she learned to wear "demure" pastel dresses as demanded by "the strategist" Gurner. Maginnis was a militant renegade and outspoken, particularly against the Catholic Church in which she was raised. Not only was she not a member of the respected medical, legal, or clerical professions, but she also regularly attacked the hypocrisy and sexism of all three. Gurner was from a Jewish family in New York. When she had her abortion, she had to rush back to her job as a bookkeeper or lose it. Phelan, who joined Maginnis in 1965, grew up poor in the South during the

Depression; at the time she joined SHA, she was married to a police officer and working as a secretary in Los Angeles.

BREAKING THE LAW

Maginnis moved from collecting petitions and lobbying to breaking the law in 1966, when California state medical authorities accused nine highly respected San Francisco physicians who had performed therapeutic abortions of participating in a criminal act. Maginnis and Gurner then decided to publicize their secret referrals to Mexican abortionists in order to provoke an arrest and generate a test case challenging the criminal abortion laws. The activists did not undertake lawbreaking lightly but felt driven to act by political events. Like everyone else who publicly urged revision of the nation's abortion laws in the early 1960s, Maginnis and Gurner were regularly approached by women and men searching for abortionists. Gurner "had a few names of people in Tijuana that she would write down on a piece of paper, and stick it in an envelope with no return address, and she would go to another town, and mail it." The secrecy of these early mailings reveals the activists' anxiety about the law. By the mid-1960s, however, bolder action seemed necessary. . . .

THE LIST

In June 1966, Maginnis passed out the first "List of Abortion Specialists" in San Francisco. In July, she escalated the attack on California law by offering to teach women how to perform their own abortions. Teaching the classes, Maginnis recalled, was one of Gurner's "brilliant" ideas. Furthermore, hoping to goad police into arresting her, Maginnis advertised her plan to give this information during an official hearing of two of the physicians under investigation for performing therapeutic abortions. Maginnis passed out leaflets, a "do-it-yourself" kit, and began conducting "classes."

Prosecutors did not pursue Maginnis in the way that she wished, but media attention garnered an immediate influx of new "sympathizers" and attracted hundreds of women clamoring for classes and the "List." By November, Maginnis and

Gurner had taught twenty-five classes in the San Francisco Bay Area and soon offered classes elsewhere in California and in Ohio, New Mexico, and Washington, D.C. Class size ranged from "15 women of various ages and race" in Berkeley to 150 in Washington, D.C. Women predominated among the "students," but men also attended. Students included people seeking abortions, reporters, and police officers; the activists welcomed all.

Although the racial, class, and educational backgrounds of the women who went to ARAL [Association for the Repeal of Abortion Laws] classes or used the "List" cannot be reconstructed, there was multiracial and cross-class support for both. The women who used ARAL represented "a very widespread cross-section of economic strata," Maginnis reports, "from destitute to rich. Poor women saved their grocery money" to pay for abortions. At an early press conference advocating legalization, Maginnis, a white woman, was joined by Audrey Smith, an African American organizer among poor Blacks in San Francisco. A Spanish-language leaflet advertised classes to San Francisco's Latina community, and Chicanas used the "List."

A NEW FEMINIST HEALTH SYSTEM

The ARAL abortion class was a model of feminist health and political education. Maginnis argued for repeal of the nation's abortion laws, taught female anatomy and reproduction, and passed around contraceptives while explaining their proper use and effectiveness. Finally, as promised, she passed out materials detailing how a woman could induce an abortion using her own fingers, gauze, syringes, and other items. However, Maginnis was never a romantic about these methods. In fact, she strongly advised against self-inducing an abortion. Foreshadowing the emphasis of the women's liberation movement on "the personal is political," Maginnis told audiences of her own self-induced abortions and subsequent hospitalizations. Not only had she had three illegal abortions, but Maginnis had also seen women injured as a result of illegal abortions and women forced to carry unwanted pregnancies to term. Furthermore,

Maginnis advised women to remain silent about their abortions and to demand a lawyer if interrogated by hospital staff or police. If a woman pursued the self-induced route, Maginnis warned, she was almost guaranteed a week in the hospital. "The cost is as much as going to Mexico," she observed. Maginnis urged her students to go to an abortion specialist instead and passed out the "List" in her classes. Plenty of women took her advice and used the "List" to find a trustworthy specialist; some met at an abortion class and went to Mexico together.

ARAL asked women who used the "List" to help with the work at the office, to write letters to their legislators, and to monitor the specialists. By asking women who had abortions to contribute in both practical and political ways, ARAL helped teach women that their need for an abortion was not only a personal problem but a political one as well. To get the "List," initially given freely, ARAL began to ask for a five-dollar contribution or two hours of work at the San Francisco office. . . .

HER LEGACY

Maginnis and her colleagues originally encouraged women to go to Mexico for abortions in order to contest existing laws in the United States. They did not plan to create an alternative feminist health system, but the numerous requests from ordinary women resulted in its creation. The "List" grew out of the quiet practice of helping individual women and publicizing it was a political strategy. As ARAL worked to protect the health of women through the inspection, supervision, and correction of practitioners; established clinics to provide basic services to the public; and educated the public and the medical profession on pregnancy and abortion, the organization became what I have called a feminist public health agency, one that always had a political purpose. In 1970, four years after the initial leafleting, the organizers observed that "the abortion laws . . . remain unrepealed, and ARAL, which was envisioned . . . as a temporary organization, is still in existence." By then, more than 12,000 women had obtained illegal abortions outside the country with ARAL's help. . . .

While lawyers challenged the law in the courtroom, ARAL defied the law publicly and daily. This feminist health organization taught women that together they could challenge and change both law and medicine, two of the most powerful social structures and professions in America. . . .

When ARAL monitored illegal abortion services . . . it aimed for more than access or safety. Maginnis and her partners wanted the medical service of abortion to be given in a caring and "humane" manner. The word *humane* was central to their vision and their activism. SHA and ARAL helped to create an expectation among women that abortion care, and, by extension, all medical care, should be provided in a sensitive fashion. Compassion was as important as expertise. In some Mexican clinics they found both. Sustaining a humane atmosphere and feminist vision in abortion clinics once the procedure was legal in the United States would prove to be equally or even more difficult than monitoring illegal practices and challenging the criminal law.

Abortion Is a Woman's Civil Right

BETTY FRIEDAN

Feminist, writer, and founder of the National Organization for Women, Betty Friedan has been at the forefront of the abortion rights movement in America. The following speech was given at the First National Conference for Repeal of Abortion Laws held in Chicago in 1969. In this speech Friedan proclaims that the time has finally come for women to claim abortion as a woman's civil right. She argues that it is a woman's fundamental right to control her own reproductive process. However, Friedan is quick to point out that women do not necessarily need to be liberated from sex, nor do they need to be liberated from motherhood. Instead, Friedan insists that only when women are allowed to be autonomous, self-determining, decision-making beings will they be free of the patriarchal shackles of motherhood. She asserts that there is a need for a sexual revolution, but argues that a revolution cannot happen without radical change.

W e are in a new stage in the sexual revolution in America. We are moving forward again, after many decades of standing still—which has been in effect to move backward. Belatedly, we have come to recognize that there is no freedom, no equality, no full human dignity and personhood possible for women until we demand control over our own bodies.

Only one voice needs to be heard on the question of whether a woman will or will not bear a child, and that is the voice of the woman herself: her own conscience, her own conscious choice. Then, and only then, will women move out of their definition as sex objects to personhood and self-determination. . . .

We are the ones to say what will happen with our bodies,

with our lives. We are finally demanding the voice that has not been accorded us, despite all the paper rights that women are supposed to have in America: all the tokenism, the lip service, the pats on the head, the sexual glamorization. The use of sex to sell everything from detergents to mouthwash, the glorification of breasts and behinds are finally being understood by women for what they are: the ultimately denigrating enshrinement of women as sex objects.

Yesterday, an obscene thing happened in the City of New York. A Committee of the State Legislature held hearings on the question of abortion. Women like me asked to testify. We were told that testimony was by invitation only. Only *one* woman was invited to testify on the question of abortion in the state of New York—a Catholic nun. The only other voices were those of men. It is obscene that men, whether they be legislators or priests or even benevolent abortion reformers, should be the only ones heard on the question of women's bodies and the reproductive process, on what happens to the people that actually bear the children in this society.

The right of woman to control her reproductive process must be established as a basic, inalienable, civil right, not to be denied or abridged by the state—just us the right of individual and religious conscience is considered an inalienable private right in both American tradition and in the American Constitution.

This is how we must address all questions governing abortion, access to birth control, and contraceptive devices. Don't talk to me about abortion reform. Abortion reform is something dreamed up by men, maybe good-hearted men, but they can only think from their male point of view. For them, women are the passive objects that somehow must be regulated; let them only have abortions for thalidomide, rape, incest. What right have they to say? What right has any man to say to any woman—you must bear this child? What right has any state to say? This is a woman's right, not a technical question needing the sanction of the state, or to be debated in terms of technicalities—they are all irrelevant.

This question can only be confronted in terms of the basic

personhood and dignity of woman, which is violated forever if she does not have the right to control her own reproductive process.

DEMANDING A VOICE: TALKING ABOUT ABORTION

It is quite remarkable what has happened in the little more than a year during which some of us have begun to talk about abortion in these terms. The people who first began talking about it loudly were women. We've had a lot of support from men, but I remember how they laughed when my group, NOW [National Organization for Women], decided that there had been enough talk about women, we wanted action; when we decided to define a new Bill of Rights for women, and one of the rights had to be the right of women to control their own reproductive process. At that time, New York State was having a constitutional convention and Larry Lader invited me to the meeting of all the different groups—church groups, medical groups, Planned Parenthood, and the rest—who were working on abortion reform. I said, we're going into the New York State constitutional convention demanding a Bill of Rights for women, and we are going to demand that it be written into the Constitution that the right of a woman to control her reproductive process must be established as a civil right, a right not to be denied or abridged by the state. Most of the people at that table, people working on abortion reform, were men. They looked at me in absolute horror, as if I was out of my mind. They said, you don't know what you are talking about, you're not an expert on this, you women have never done anything like this. You're just going to rock the boat—this isn't the way to go about it—you listen to us: . . . A.C.L.U. [American Civil Liberties Union], the clergymen, the medical people.

If I were easily intimidated, I would have slunk out. But I said well, you may be right but as far as we are concerned, this is the only way that abortion is worth talking about; we're going to demand it and let's see what happens. As I left, a couple of the women who were sitting quietly at the table came up and said, "We'd like to help." Then, lo and behold, I began to hear ministers and A.D.A. and A.C.L.U. and others begin to voice the same position, in terms of woman's basic right. We began to get to the nitty-gritty of it. In the rest of this conference, you can talk about all the technical reasons that different abortion reform laws are inadequate or have worked or haven't worked. It's hardly interesting. What interests me is the basic position, and the resonance it gives to the whole revolution toward sexual equality today.

BECOMING VISIBLE

Women, even though they're almost too visible as sex objects in this country, are invisible people. As the Negro was the invisible man, so women are the invisible people in America today: we must now become visible women who have a share in the decisions of the mainstream of government, of politics, of the church—who don't just cook the church supper, but preach the sermon; who don't just look up the ZIP codes and address the envelopes, but make the political decisions; who don't just do the housework of industry, but make some of the executive decisions. Women, above all, who say what their own lives and personalities are going to be, and no longer listen to or even permit male experts to define what "feminine" is or isn't.

The essence of the denigration of women is our definition as sex object. To confront our inequality, therefore, we must confront both society's denigration of us in these terms and our own self-denigration as people.

Am I saying that women must be liberated from sex? No. I am saying that sex will only be liberated to be a human dialogue, sex will only cease to be a sniggering, dirty joke and an obsession in this society, when women become active self-determining people, liberated to a creativity beyond motherhood, to a full human creativity.

Am I saying that women must be liberated from motherhood? No. I am saying that motherhood will only be a joyous and responsible human act when women are free to make, with full conscious choice and full human responsibility, the decisions to become mothers. Then, and only then, will they be able to embrace motherhood without conflict, when they will be able to define themselves not just as somebody's mother, not just as servants of children, not just as breeding receptacles, but as people for whom motherhood is a freely chosen part of life, freely celebrated while it lasts, but for whom creativity has many more dimensions, as it has for men.

Then, and only then, will motherhood cease to be a curse and a chain for men and for children. For despite all the lip service paid to motherhood today, all the roses sent on Mother's Day, all

Betty Friedan, founder of the National Organization for Women, tells reporters that their organization intends to "put sex into section 1" of the New York State constitution.

the commercials and the hypocritical ladies' magazines' celebration of women in their roles as housewives and mothers, the fact is that all television or night-club comics have to do is go before a microphone and say the words "my wife," and the whole audience erupts into gales of guilty, vicious and obscene laughter. . . .

Motherhood is a bane almost by definition, or at least partly so, as long as women are forced to be mothers—and only mothers—against their will. Like a cancer cell living its life through another cell, women today are forced to live too much through their children and husbands (they are too dependent on them, and therefore are forced to take too much varied resentment, vindictiveness, inexpressable resentment and rage out on their husbands and children). . . .

Am I saying that women have to be liberated from men? That men are the enemy? No. I am saying the *men* will only be truly liberated to love women and to be fully themselves when women are liberated to have a full say in the decisions of their lives and their society.

Until that happens, men are going to bear the guilty burden of the passive destiny they have forced upon women, the suppressed resentment, the sterility of love when it is not between two fully active, joyous people, but has in it the element of exploitation. And men will not be free to be all they can be as long as they must live up to an image of masculinity that disallows all the tenderness and sensitivity in a man, all that might be considered feminine. Men have enormous capacities in them that they have to repress and fear in order to live up to the obsolete, brutal, bear-killing, Ernest Hemingway, crew-cut Prussian, napalm-all-the-children in-Vietnam, bang-bang-you're-dead image of masculinity. Men are not allowed to admit that they sometimes are afraid. They are not allowed to express their own sensitivity, their own need to be passive sometimes and not always active. Men are not allowed to cry. So they are only half-human, as women are only half-human, until we can go this next step forward. All the burdens and responsibilities that men are supposed to shoulder alone makes them, I think, resent women's pedestal, much as that pedestal may be a burden for women.

Talking About a Revolution

This is the real sexual revolution. Not the cheap headlines in the papers about at what age boys and girls go to bed with each other and whether they do it with or without the benefit of marriage. That's the least of it. The real sexual revolution is the emergence of women from passivity, from the point where they are the easiest victims for all the seductions, the waste, the worshiping of false gods in our affluent society, to full self-determination and full dignity. And it is the emergence of men from the stage where they are inadvertent brutes and masters to sensitive, complete humanity.

This revolution cannot happen without radical changes in the family as we know it today; in our concepts of marriage and love, in our architecture, our cities, our theology, our politics, our art. Not that women are special. Not that women are superior. But these expressions of human creativity are bound to be infinitely more various and enriching when women and men are allowed to relate to each other beyond the strict confines of the *Ladies' Home Journal*'s definition of the Mamma and Papa marriage.

If we are finally allowed to become full people, not only will children be born and brought up with more love and responsibility than today, but we will break out of the confines of that sterile little suburban family to relate to each other in terms of all of the possible dimensions of our personalities—male and female, as comrades, as colleagues, as friends, as lovers. And without so much hate and jealousy and buried resentment and hypocrisies, there will be a whole new sense of love that will make what we call love on Valentine's Day look very pallid.

It's crucial, therefore, that we see this question of abortion as more than a quantitative move, more than a politically expedient move. Abortion repeal is not a question of political expediency. It is part of something greater. It is historic that we are addressing ourselves this weekend to perhaps its first national confrontation by women and men. Women's voices are finally being heard aloud, saying it the way it is about the question of abortion both in its most basic sense of morality and in its new political sense as part of the unfinished revolution of sexual equality.

In this confrontation, we are making an important milestone in this marvelous revolution that began long before any of us here were born and which still has a long way to go. As the pioneers from Mary Wollstonecraft to Margaret Sanger gave us the consciousness that brought us from our several directions here, so we here, in changing the very terms of the debate on abortion to assert woman's right to choose, and to define the terms of our lives ourselves, move women further to full human dignity. Today, we moved history forward.

An Early Abortion Counseling Service Advertises Its Services

Chicago Women's Liberation Union

The Abortion Counseling Service, also known as "Jane," was an organization affiliated with the Chicago Women's Liberation Union. The main purpose of the organization was to provide safe, affordable, and accessible abortions to women in need. The following excerpt is taken from an original informational brochure. In this brochure, the mission of the organization is laid out; it encourages all women to get involved in Jane and to help secure equal opportunities and the right to safe and legal abortions for women. The brochure asserts that only women can bring about their own liberation, and it is therefore women's responsibility to create the much-needed legal and social change.

WHAT IS THE ABORTION COUNSELING SERVICE?

We are women whose ultimate goal is the liberation of women in society. One important way we are working toward that goal is by helping any woman who wants an abortion to get one as safely and cheaply as possible under existing conditions.

Abortion is a safe, simple, relatively painless operation when performed by a trained person in clean conditions. In fact, it's less complicated than a tonsillectomy. People hear about its horrors because desperate women turn to incompetent people or

Chicago Women's Liberation Union, "Abortion—a Woman's Decision, a Woman's Right," www.cwluherstory.com.

resort to unsafe methods. Much of our time is spent finding reliable and sympathetic doctors who will perform safe abortions for as little money as possible. You will receive the best medical care we know of.

Although abortions are illegal in Illinois, the state has not brought charges against any woman who has had an abortion. Only those who perform abortions have been prosecuted.

Any information you give your counselor is kept confidential. She will not give your name to anyone or discuss anything you tell her without your permission. It is vitally important that you are completely honest about your medical history with your counselor and the doctor.

Loan Fund

Because abortions are illegal and in such demand, they are exorbitantly expensive. In fact, an abortion frequently costs as much as the combined doctor and hospital bills for having a baby. The ACS [Abortion Counseling Service] believes that no woman should be denied an abortion because she is unable to pay for it. We have a small and constantly depleted noninterest loan fund for women who would otherwise be unable to have an abortion. It is non-profit and non-discriminatory. Twenty-five dollars of what you pay for an abortion goes toward maintaining this service. If you receive money from this fund, please repay it as promptly as you can so that the money may be used to help other women. An unpaid loan may mean that we cannot lend money to someone else who needs it desperately . . .

Abortion Is a Social Problem

We are giving our time not only because we want to make abortions safer, cheaper and more accessible for the individual women who come to us, but because we see the whole abortion issue as a problem of society. The current abortion laws are a symbol of the sometimes subtle, but often blatant, oppression of women in our society.

Women should have the right to control their own bodies and lives. Only a woman who is pregnant can determine whether she has enough resources—economic, physical and emotional—at a given time to bear and rear a child. Yet at present the decision to bear the child or have an abortion is taken out of her hands by governmental bodies which can have only the slightest notion of the problems involved.

Cultural, moral and religious feelings are largely against abortion, and society does all it can to make a woman feel guilty and degraded if she has one.

The same society that denies a woman the decision not to have a child refuses to provide humane alternatives for women who do have children, such as child care facilities to permit the mother to work, or role flexibility so that men can share in the raising of children. The same society that insists that women should and do find their basic fulfillment in motherhood will condemn the unwed mother and her fatherless child.

The same society that glamorizes women as sex objects and teaches them from early childhood to please and satisfy men views pregnancy and childbirth as punishment for "immoral" or "careless" sexual activity, especially if the woman is uneducated, poor or black. The same morality that says "that's what she gets for fooling around" also fails to recognize society's responsibility to the often unwelcome child that results. Punitive welfare laws reflect this view, and churches reinforce it.

Our society's version of equal opportunity means that lower-class women bear unwanted children or face expensive, illegal and often unsafe abortions, while well-connected middle-class women can frequently get safe and hush-hush "D and Cs" in hospitals.

Only women can bring about their own liberation. It is time for women to get together to change the male-made laws and to aid their sisters caught in the bind of legal restrictions and social stigma. Women must fight together to change the attitudes of society about abortion and to make the state provide free abortions as a human right.

There are currently many groups lobbying for population control, legal abortion and selective sterilization. Some are actually attempting to control some populations, prevent some births—for instance those of black people or poor people. We are opposed to these or any form of genocide. We are for every woman having exactly as many children as she wants, when she wants, if she wants. It's time the Bill of Rights applied to women. It's time women got together and started really fighting for their rights. Governments have to be made to realize that abortions are part of the health care they must provide for the people who support them.

If you are interested in giving your energy and time to help bring about a better life for yourself and your daughters and sons, get in touch with Jane.

Organizing Illegal Abortion Services: A First-Hand Account

RUTH SURGAL AND THE CWLU HERSTORY COMMITTEE

The following interview is with Ruth Surgal, a woman's rights activist who was an influential leader of Jane. Sponsored by the Chicago Women's Liberation Union (CWLU) from 1969 to 1973, Jane helped women obtain illegal abortions by establishing networks and training lay people to perform abortion procedures. Hundreds of women, including political activists, scientists, steelworkers, and students, volunteered for the CWLU and worked to create personal and societal transformation.

Ruth Surgal describes her participation in the clandestine organization in the late 1960s and early 1970s at the height of illegal abortions and pro-choice activism. She explains why she participated in the organization, the makeup of the organization, and the hardships that she and the other volunteers encountered due to the nature of their work. In explaining her experience, she draws on the connection between feminism and abortion counseling and the never-ending struggle to achieve and retain woman's rights.

> Now originally, way back in the beginning, I really thought feminism was stupid. It's really embarrassing to think about it. But, I was at a Women for Peace meeting and some women came to talk about the women's movement and feminism. I just thought they were you know, having trouble in their marriages . . . none of it made any sense to me.
>
> —Ruth Surgal, 1999

Ruth Surgal and the CWLU Herstory Committee, "Organizing a Clandestine Abortion Service," www.cwluherstory.com, October 11, 2004. Reproduced by permission.

... Soon after her first puzzled encounter with feminist ideas, Ruth Surgal had one of those "Ah" or "Click" experiences, when suddenly, women's liberation made perfect sense. Many women had such experiences in the 1960's and 1970's. For Ruth it was listening to a 1969 radio interview with Marlene Dixon, a University of Chicago professor who had been fired because of her outspoken support of the women's liberation movement.

Active in the anti-war movement, Surgal felt the need to do something different.

> I was looking for something to do because I was not willing to get arrested in the anti-war movement. It wasn't that I didn't care about it, but for whatever reason it wasn't my personal fight. And I knew that the women's movement was my personal fight and that I would be willing to go to the wall for it, or whatever, get arrested—not that I did, but ... I went to this house and there were different activities, you know, different things that were being organized.

> There was the Women's Union, there probably was daycare, there might have been some sports, a newsletter, and an abortion counseling service. And since I was a social worker, and I knew crisis intervention, that was of course what I would do. So it didn't come out of a particular interest in abortion. It came out of my work experience.

THE BEGINNING: LESSONS LEARNED

Jane began as a referral service, but for Surgal and the others, dealing with the actual male abortionists was a very frustrating experience. There were blindfolds, high prices, secret motel rooms and the nagging feeling that women needed to be in control over the process. Finally the Service settled on one abortionist who seemed more flexible than the rest. Claiming to be a physician, he became known as "Mike". Although no one questioned his technical expertise as an abortionist, it was eventually learned that Mike really wasn't a doctor. . . .

According to Ruth, Mike was a very complicated person:

> He was a con man. I mean he truly, truly, truly was a con

man. Back in the days of the counseling service I thought he was the sexiest man I ever met. It was like I could hardly stand it, I thought he was—it was just impossible. You know, that's how I felt. I just thought the sexiest person. He was just exuding it. . . .

But he thought I was a traitor so to speak, a stool pigeon because I was the person who insisted that we had to let everybody know that he wasn't a real doctor. And he was furious and he yelled and screamed and was just beside himself and I felt bad.

While working for Jane, Mike taught people his abortion techniques. As people learned what he knew, the blindfolds began coming off and the prices dropped. The people he trained, trained others, so that after his departure, Jane became an all-woman service.

"EMPOWERMENT"

Jane's medical techniques were very good, but Jane always felt that technical knowledge wasn't enough. The women seeking the abortions needed to feel that they were part of the process. Although the modern term "empowerment" has become something of a threadbare politician's cliche, Jane actually took the idea seriously.

Counselors and intake personnel learned to listen to Jane's clients carefully, as what was NOT said was often as important as what WAS said. Women were encouraged to talk about themselves and their lives. People talked about women's liberation, about how women were expected to be sexy and desirable, but then were punished for becoming pregnant. Women were encouraged to talk about their personal experiences with children, pregnancy and abortion. Jane wanted to demystify the abortion experience so that people could make intelligent decisions about what to do.

Surgal explains:

It was one of the things we talked about a lot that we were not doing something TO this woman, we were doing something WITH this woman and she was as much a part of it, and part of the process as we were. So that we would talk about how we relied on them if we got busted. You know we would explain that they were not doing anything illegal. We were doing something illegal. But we need their help, and you know don't talk about it, and we have to be quiet, and it might be a terrible way to do things but this is what we have to do. And people were pretty good.

THE MAKEUP OF THE ORGANIZATION: A PLACE FOR EVERYONE

Jane was a diverse group of people and styles varied:

Some people were much more political and could get really good political discussions going. Others would just kinda sit, and there'd be friendly conversations. You know it just really depended on who it was. I mean people were helpful to each other by and large. Not necessarily in really big ways. One person would have an abortion and then the next person would, just like when you go to the dentist, [and say things like] oh you know it wasn't that bad. People were pretty good. But not always. . . . I think because we set it up in such a comfortable way, and we tried so hard to be respectful.

I think that that kind of attitude of respect and egalitarian or equality or whatever the word is, helps people be together, and bonds people. You know, I think mostly people recognized real support, you know, and the kind of warmth and acceptance, whatever it is that comes from that sorta approach and a way of—I suppose people have different styles, I made myself so present, that was my way of doing it, that I, you know, to make people comfortable I'd make myself present in a, at least this is what I think I did, in a way that was strong and vulnerable at the same time.

Jane tried to find places for volunteers based on their skills and abilities. Surgal herself did not feel confident enough to perform the actual abortion procedure:

I think in the beginning I was curious about the process. But because I am so strongly a helping person there was somebody who's hand had to be held and there I was to do it. . . .

Then actually helping a little bit, or actually trying to do abortions, I really had a lot of trouble with that. I could do the first part. I could dilate the cervix, I could give the shot, but I couldn't do that abortion. I could do it now. But I couldn't do it then. And now I could do it because I trust my hands. And then I didn't. And I trust them now because of doing pottery. Like I couldn't make pie crusts before and now I can.

I was afraid I would hurt somebody. If I couldn't see what my hands were doing, how did I know? As long as I could see what I was doing I was Ok, but once I had to go inside and I couldn't see anymore, I had no confidence that I would do it right.

Surgal decided that her talents would better serve the group as "Big Jane", the term that was used to describe the person who actually assigned abortion counselors, scheduled abortions and was the members' main source of information. She explains:

I took the job of Big Jane, that was the only other seriously powerful position. And I did it. And now, I was fortunate, or I should say the group was fortunate. There was a person who was doing Big Jane and she was not doing a very good job, and she was very good at doing abortions. So I said all right we're switching, I'm going do this and you're going do that, and I could do that because I had the power in the group to do it. Although everybody was angry, but they wouldn't tell me about it because I had the power and I could do it. You know how that goes.

THE "ABORTION 7": LEGAL ENFORCEMENT INTERVENES

Decision making within Jane could be difficult. Conditions were stressful because of the life and death nature of the work they were doing, the necessity for secrecy and the knowledge that they had to focus on the work because so many desperate women depended on them. People had a tendency to suppress open disagreement to keep the group united and task oriented. Naturally, this created its own problems, but when 7 Jane members were unexpectedly arrested and the very existence of the group was threatened, people continued performing abortions, even as disagreements about strategy intensified. . . .

Jane soon figured out the arrests were not part of an overall plan to shut down the Abortion Counseling Service, but rather the actions of an individual police commander. Ironically, some of Jane's clients came from police families and the overall attitude of the usually repressive and controlling Mayor Richard J. Daley city administration was to unofficially ignore Jane's activities.

Not long after the *Roe vrs. Wade* decision legalized abortion in January of 1973, the case against the "Abortion 7" was quietly dropped. Some Jane members wanted to go on, believing that legalization did not address the issues of cost and the quality of care. Others were burned out, or feared that because abortion was now legally profitable, the medical establishment would have them prosecuted for practicing medicine without a license.

LOOKING FORWARD

Ruth Surgal hoped that Jane's extensive experience in performing abortions would become a model:

> I was naïve, I thought we had learned in the counseling service how to deliver services in a very respectful way that made it so much easier on everybody, and particularly for the woman. We could go out into the world and the medical world would take it and everybody would then practice medicine differently. Well, you know, of course wasn't going to happen. I mean even in abortion clinics it didn't happen, so, I was naïve.

Jane closed its doors in the spring of 1973. The Abortion Counseling Service existed in tumultuous times and no one who went through Jane was unaffected by the intensity of the experience.

For the people who I know, it was the single most intense period of our life and when it stopped there was something missing. And you couldn't find anything to do that carried quite that energy for a long time. I mean, how often to get a chance to actually do something that's not enormously complicated and is truly helpful, you know. You can be helpful in lots of ways, but this was really helpful because without us they would've been in serious trouble. These were people who couldn't afford to go to all the regular places, you know, for abortion. Or the places they went to they would get hurt. So what we did was really important. Doesn't happen very often in a lifetime. Or hardly at all, you know that one gets a chance to do that.

It would be all too easy to romanticize Jane, and make its members larger than life. Ruth Surgal cautions against "overvaluing" the Jane experience because, "It makes it outside of normal experience, and it isn't outside of normal experience."

Jane members decided they had a job to do and they did it. When the job was over, Jane members moved on with their diverse lives.

Today Ruth Surgal is still involved with social work and is an accomplished potter. The hands that she feared were not steady enough to perform actual abortions, today shape clay into exquisitely subtle forms.

She is an active member of the Herstory Website Project and patiently continues to give interviews about her participation in Jane, explaining how she feels about it now:

It's only afterwards that you think about it. You know, thinking about it now I think about that, how lucky I was to have had that experience. But at the time it was just something you did, because you wanted to. It wasn't a big deal. It didn't feel like, oh I'm doing this really important thing. It didn't feel like that at all. It just was another job to do. Afterwards it felt important . . . you know, and even though it was just this little tiny world important, still it had this number of women and it was a helpful thing to do.

I Had an Illegal Abortion

ELEANOR COONEY

The following selection is taken from Eleanor Cooney's article first published in *Mother Jones* magazine. In this article Cooney describes her experience as an unmarried pregnant teenager in the 1960s searching for the resources to have an abortion. She takes the reader on her journey from college in Boston to a friend's couch in New York City. She visits seedy clinic after seedy clinic while her desperation and frustration grow greater. Cooney draws readers in and forces them to feel her panic. Her story implores readers to learn from her experience and mobilize to create much needed social and political change. She begs readers to become educated and to educate others about abortion rights in order to create a society where having an abortion does not expose a woman to the danger of being raped or robbed. She maintains that it is the responsibility of all to keep the back-alley abortionists out of business and to ensure women have rights to protect themselves against injustice.

In 1959, when I was a precocious smarty-pants still in grade school, I wrote a fake letter to Doris Blake, the *New York Daily News* advice columnist. I pretended to be a teenage girl "in trouble." I spun a tale of a liquor-soaked prom night and passing out in the back of a car. I included a cast of entirely fictional characters—a worthless boyfriend, a mentally unstable mother, a strict, brutal father. I ended my letter with: "Now I think I am pregnant. Please help me. I am desperate."

I'm not sure what I expected, but my letter was not printed, and no advice was forthcoming. The silence was utter. Possibly Miss Blake, like Nathanael West's Miss Lonelyhearts, had a drawer where such letters were tossed. If so, the other letters in that drawer were no doubt a lot like mine—except that they were not written by wiseass children. They were real. And for the writers of those letters, the silence was real. And I remember thinking: *Gee*, what if I really were that girl I made up? What would I do?

One summer night some years later, when I was not quite 18, I got knocked up. There was nothing exciting or memorable or even interestingly sordid about the sex. I wasn't raped or coerced, nor was I madly in love or drunk or high. The guy was another kid, actually younger than I, just a friend, and it pretty much happened by default. We were horny teenagers with nothing else to do.

Nature, the ultimate unsentimental pragmatist, has its own notions about what constitutes a quality liaison. What nature wants is for sperm and egg to meet, as often as possible, whenever and wherever possible. Whatever it takes to expedite that meeting is fine with nature. If it's two people with a bassinet and a nursery all decorated and waiting and a shelf full of baby books, fine. If it's a 12-year-old girl who's been married off to a 70-year-old Afghan chieftain, fine. And if it's a couple of healthy young oafs like my friend and me, who knew perfectly well where babies come from but just got stupid for about 15 minutes, that's fine, too.

In the movies, newly pregnant women trip, fall down the stairs, and "lose the baby." Ah. If only it were that easy. In real life, once that egg is fertilized and has glided on down the fallopian tube, selected its nesting place, and settled in, it's notoriously secure, behaves like visiting royalty. Nature doesn't give a fig about the hostess's feelings of hospitality or lack of them. If the zygote's not defective, and the woman is in good health, almost nothing will shake it loose. Anyone who's been pregnant and didn't want to be knows this is so. . . .

Too Far Gone

By the middle of September, I'd missed two periods and my cigarettes were tasting peculiar. I was bound for freshman year at college in Boston, though, so I just ignored the facts and went off to school. It took a third missed period and almost throwing up in the backseat of a car packed with kids to penetrate my adolescent thickheadedness.

I had a savvy friend in New York, Kat, who only dated rich older men. I figured she'd be the one to call. Soon a long ride on buses and trains took me out to a house in a Boston suburb. The doctor's wife answered the door. There was no waiting room, no magazines, no other patients. The house was completely ordinary, perhaps a touch run-down. She showed me into a room off the front hall and vanished.

Except for a small sink, the office was just a regular room, a parlor, with green walls and venetian blinds and a worn rug on the floor. A tall, battered, glass-doored porcelain cabinet stood in a corner. Through the glass, I could see on the shelves a dusty disorderly jumble of stethoscopes, hypodermics, bottles, little rubber hammers, basins, forceps, clamps, speculums, wads of cotton. There were rust stains in the sink and a tired old examining table.

The doctor, a little nervous man with glasses and a bald head, came in. I explained my problem. I have to examine you, he said. And he said: Everything has to be clean, very clean. He went to the sink and washed and washed his hands.

He finished and stood there without saying anything. His eyes were sort of glittering behind his glasses, and he acted as if I was supposed to know what to do next. I glanced around for a gown, but he was looking impatient, so I just took off my underwear and climbed onto the table.

He didn't bother with a glove. He poked around a while, then told me that I'd waited too long, I was too far gone, it would be too risky for him, and that would be $25.

And I was back out on the suburban street, the door shut firmly behind me.

THE BIG CITY

Kat told me to come to New York and bring $500. I slept on the couch in her apartment. Kat's roommate, Elaine, gave me the address of a doctor over in Jersey City. I took a train and walked 10 blocks to a street of old brownstones, some of them with their windows boarded up. There had been no calling ahead for an "appointment"; you were supposed to just show up.

This doctor had a waiting room, with dark walls and a very high ceiling, the front room of the brownstone. It was full of people, facing each other along opposite walls, sitting in old, cracked, brown leather parlor chairs with stand-up ashtrays here and there, like in a bus station. A set of tall sliding wooden doors stood closed between that room and the next. Everyone was smoking, including me. The air was blue.

Several Puerto Rican-looking women chattered away in Spanish and seemed perfectly cheerful. There were a few men, who looked as if they might be accompanying somebody, and some more women who sat silent and staring.

And there was a couple who stood out like a pair of borzoi among street mutts: a man and woman, tall, slim, expensively dressed WASPs [white Anglo-Saxon Protestants], faces grim, looking like people who'd taken a seriously wrong turn off the highway. I remember feeling sorry for them.

The tall wooden doors separated. A potbellied man in shirt-sleeves who resembled Harpo Marx minus the fun stood there. His eyes moved around the room. He looked at the Puerto Rican women, the tall WASP woman, then at me, then the WASP woman again, considered for a moment, turned back to me, and pointed.

You, he said.

I got up and went in. He slid the doors shut. We were alone.

The windows in here had been nailed over with plywood, and the floor was ancient linoleum. There was a smell of insecticide. Boxes and bundles of paper were piled high in the dim corners and on a rolltop desk, and along the walls were shelves crammed messily with stethoscopes, hypodermics, speculums. The examining table was the centerpiece of the room, antique and massive, from the last century, dark green leather, steel and ceramic, designed so that the patient did not lie flat but in a semi-reclining position. Instead of stirrups, there were obstetrical leg supports. A tall old-fashioned floor lamp with a rose silk shade and a fringe, the only light in the room, stood next to the table alongside a cylinder of gas. An unlit crystal chandelier dangled in the overhead shadows.

The doctor had a trace of some sort of European accent. German, I guessed. He was about a foot shorter than I was, and behaved with obsequious deference, as if I had dropped in for an afternoon sherry. He gestured toward the examining table with a courtly flourish. I sat between the leg supports while he stood close and asked questions: Last period, how many times had I had sex, was I married, how many men had I had sex with, did they have large or small penises, were they circumcised, what positions, did I like it?

He moved the floor lamp closer. I put my legs in the apparatus and looked up at the chandelier.

He didn't bother with a glove, either. He thrust several fingers in, hard, so I could feel the scrape of his nails.

Ouch! I said politely.

Ouch, he mocked. Never mind your ouch. He pushed his fingers in harder and pressed down on my belly with his other hand.

You are very far along, he said. It will be a very difficult procedure. Come back tomorrow. Be here at seven o'clock in the evening. Give me one hundred dollars now because this will be difficult. You can pay the rest when you come back. Bring cash. Five hundred more.

I borrowed the extra hundred from Kat, and enlisted someone I knew to ride out to Jersey City with me on the train, a guy who was something of an ex-boyfriend. Even though I was enigmatic about why we were going to Jersey City at night, he guessed what was up, and seemed fairly entertained at the prospect.

This time, there was no one in the waiting room. The doctor looked very annoyed when he saw that I wasn't alone. My friend stayed out there while I went into the office. The doctor locked the door behind us.

When I was on the table, he stood between my legs and

pressed and ground his pelvis against me and then put his fingers in for a while.

Then he said: You are too far gone. I cannot do it.

I put my legs down and sat up. He stood next to me, leaned on me heavily, and rubbed his two hands up my thigh, all the way up, so that his fingertips collided with my crotch. I understood then that he'd known perfectly well on my last visit that he wasn't going to go through with it.

You are a beautiful girl, a beautiful girl, he breathed moistly onto my face as his hands slid up and down, up and down. It is too late. Take my advice. Have the baby. Have the baby.

He unlocked the sliding doors and beckoned my friend in.

Get married, he said. Have the baby.

Hey, I'm not the guy, said my friend.

What about my hundred dollars? I asked.

Get out of here, the doctor said, and turned his back.

When we got to my friend's train stop, he walked off whistling a jaunty tune. Good luck, he said, and was gone. . . .

ASKING FOR HELP

The day after I returned from Jersey City, there was another doctor in a seedy little basement office in New York, who didn't even touch me. He said the only way to do it at this point would be to perform a miniature caesarean, not something he could do in his office.

Kat and Elaine were plainly getting tired of having me and my problem on their couch. They came up with a phone number in Florida. I called. A male voice said I should fly to Miami. They'd meet me and take me to one of the islands, to a clinic. Give us the telephone number of where you're staying now in New York. We'll call you back and confirm the arrangements.

He called back within an hour. It was set: Fly to Miami next Thursday, between the hours of noon and five. Wear something bright red so we'll know you when you get off the plane. And bring eight hundred dollars, in cash.

One last thing, he said. You must not tell anyone where you're going.

They understand that I'm over three months, right? I said.

Yeah, yeah. They know. It's all set.

I hung up. This didn't feel good at all. Florida, the islands, wads of cash, distant voices.

I thought about doing what I should have done in the first place: calling my mother.

Not calling her in the beginning wasn't because my mother was a prude or anything like that. Hardly. It was because I was naturally secretive, had wanted to take care of things on my own. I just wanted it to go away. But there was a limit to even my pigheadedness. I thought about how sad it would make my mother if I just disappeared. My mother, who was right there in the city, swung into action instantly. She made arrangements with a doctor she knew, and borrowed the $1,500 it would cost because of the added risk.

This doctor had a clean, modern office in Midtown. He drew a diagram showing the difference between a first-trimester D&C and what I'd be having. After three months, he said, the placenta and the blood vessels that feed it grow too complex to simply be scraped out. To do so would be to just about guarantee a hemorrhage. In a normal birth or miscarriage, he said, the uterus contracts, shearing off the placenta and pinching off the connecting blood vessels. We induce a miscarriage, he said, by injecting a saline solution into the amniotic sac. The fetus dies. The uterus rejects it by contracting. That way, no hemorrhage. Then we go in and take it out. If it were done any other way, it could easily kill you.

A date was made for the following week. I was off of Kat and Elaine's couch and on my mother's.

One evening, my mother's phone rang. It was the man in Florida. He'd tracked me down through Kat, and he was angry. What the hell had happened? Where was I? They'd waited all day at the airport in Miami, met every plane. I apologized, told him I'd made other arrangements here at home. He said I was a f—ing bitch who owed money to him and a lot of other people, told me to go f— myself, and hung up.

Maybe everything would have been peachy if I'd gone to the

islands. Maybe I'd have come back with a tan and heartwarming stories of kindness and caring that I'd remember fondly through the years. A rather different picture always comes to mind, though, and it involves a morgue in a run-down little hospital with heat and flies, and then a dinghy with an outboard, or maybe a fishing boat with a rumbling, smoky diesel engine, heading out into the Caribbean at night bearing a largish canvas bag weighted with cinder blocks. . . .

That year in the 1960s, several thousand American women were treated in emergency rooms for botched abortions, and there were at least 200 known deaths. Comparing my story with others from the pre-*Roe* era, what impresses me is how close I veered to mortal danger in spite of not living under most of the usual terrible strictures. Unlike so many of the women I've read about and talked to, especially the teenagers, I was quite unburdened by shame and guilt, I'd never, ever had the "nice girls don't do it" trip laid on me. I came from a religion-free background. I wasn't worried in the least about "sin," was not at all ambivalent about whether abortion was right or wrong. I wasn't sheltered or ignorant. I didn't face parental disapproval or stigmatization of any kind. I had no angry husband. My mother would have leapt in and helped me at any point. There was no need at all to keep my condition secret and to procrastinate, but I did it anyway. What does this say about how it was for other young girls and women who didn't have my incredible luck? I was luckier than most in another department, too—being raped by the abortionist was a major hazard of the era. I merely got diddled by a couple of disgusting old men. It was nasty and squalid, but certainly didn't kill me. As I said, I got off easy. . . .

SOCIAL RESPONSIBILITY

Women of all kinds seek and have always sought abortion: married, single, in their twenties, thirties, and forties, teenagers. Some have no children, some have several already. Some never want children, some want children later. They are churchgoers, atheists, agnostics. They are morally upright pillars of the community, they are prostitutes. They're promiscuous, they're monogamous, they're recent virgins. They get pregnant under all kinds of circumstances: consensual sex, nonconsensual sex, sex that falls somewhere between consensual and nonconsensual. Some are drunk or using drugs, some never even touch an aspirin. Some use no birth control, some use birth control that fails.

The desperate teenager I invented in my letter to Doris Blake in 1959 surely had hundreds, maybe thousands, of real-life counterparts at the very moment I put the envelope in the mail. All kinds of women are vulnerable and are affected by the particulars of abortion law, but the ones most profoundly affected are the very young, and it's a one-two punch from both nature and society. First, nature itself conspires to make teenagers defenseless—they're lushly fertile, their brains are flooded with sex hormones, and their judgment, practical knowledge, and common sense have been known to be less than perfect.

Teenagers—especially those who are poor and uneducated—are by far the group having the most elective late-term abortions. If we truly wish to protect the young and vulnerable, . . . then we must make teenage girls a top priority. Make sure they don't get pregnant in the first place, and not just by preaching "abstinence only." If they do get pregnant, don't throw a net of fear, confusion, and complication over them that will only cause them to hide their conditions for as long as they can. Because that's exactly what they'll do. You could argue that "partial-birth" abortion is the price a society pays when it calculatedly keeps teenage girls ignorant instead of aggressively arming them with the facts of life and, if necessary, the equipment to protect themselves from pregnancy.

I was hardly one of those tragically vulnerable teenagers. I suppose I was the kind of wanton female the lawmakers and wrath-of-God types look down on. There's no doubt that I was stupid and irresponsible, and I certainly knew better than what you might have surmised from my actions. By some standards, I suppose you could say I was a slut. Those sleazy doctors left no doubt that that's how they saw me. Some would say I got what I deserved, or that I deserved to die.

The arguments would be endless, but they would be irrelevant to the facts. From the moment I started looking for an abortion, not once did I even consider going through with the pregnancy. Not for one second. It simply was not going to happen. Nothing, and I mean nothing, was going to stop me, and it could have cost me my life. And this is what I had in common with millions and millions of women throughout time and history. When a woman does not want to be pregnant, the drive to become unpregnant can turn into a force equal to the nature that wants her to stay pregnant. And then she *will* look for an abortion, whether it's legal or illegal, clean or filthy, safe or riddled with danger. This is simply a fact, whatever our opinion of it. And whether we like it or not, humans, married and unmarried, will continue to have sex—wisely, foolishly, violently, nicely, hostilely, pleasantly, dangerously, responsibly, carelessly, sordidly, exaltedly—and there will be pregnancies: wanted, unwanted, partly wanted, partly unwanted.

A society that does not accept the facts is a childish society, and a society that makes abortion illegal . . . is a cruel and backward society that makes being female a crime. It works in partnership with the illegal abortionist. It puts him in business, sends him his customers, and employs him to dispense crude, dirty, barbaric, savage punishment to those who break the law. And the ones who are punished by the illegal abortionist are always women: mothers, sisters, daughters, wives.

It's no way to treat a lady.

CHAPTER 3

A TURNING POINT: *ROE V. WADE* AND ITS AFTERMATH

AMERICAN
SOCIAL
MOVEMENTS

I Won *Roe v. Wade*

SARAH WEDDINGTON

Sarah Weddington has had a long and successful career as an attorney, legislator, professor, and author. At the age of twenty-seven she successfully argued for the legalization of abortion in the historic *Roe v. Wade* case in front of the U.S. Supreme Court. She has spent her entire professional career serving as an advocate for women. She served three terms in the Texas House of Representatives, was appointed the U.S. Department of Agriculture's general counsel, and was the assistant to the president of the United States during the Carter Administration.

In 1992 Weddington penned *A Question of Choice* from which the following is excerpted. Weddington describes the obstacles and victories she encountered as a woman fighting for choice. The following selection explains in detail Weddington's reaction to the news that she had won *Roe v. Wade* and her interpretation of the Supreme Court's decision. Although she had secured a woman's right to choose, she knew that the struggle was not over, and that the movement's next step would be to protect its victory.

On January 19 [1973], I filed my first legislative package, the proposed changes to the Texas abortion law. Included were a bill to authorize pregnant females aged sixteen or older to consent to abortion, a bill providing that only a woman's consent (and not that of her husband) was needed for her own sterilization, and a bill allowing doctors to give contraceptives to women under eighteen without parental involvement.

The next day, a Saturday, [my husband] Ron and I watched on television the inauguration of Richard Nixon to his second term as president. We groused and talked about throwing biscuits at the screen. We discussed again the rumor that Nixon did not want the "Nixon Court" deciding the abortion cases while he was running for reelection; we wondered how long it would be before the Supreme Court announced its decision.

VICTORY!

Monday, January 22, was wet and wintry, the kind of day I wished I could stay in bed and read a book. Nonetheless, I went to the Capitol early to get organized for the week and catch up on correspondence. Ruth Bowers came by my office to visit over coffee before she set out to deliver pro-choice literature to all the legislators. Shortly after nine in Austin, at our law office at home, [my colleague] Martha Davis took a call from a *New York Times* reporter. "May I speak to Mrs. Weddington?" he asked. Martha explained I was at the Capitol. "Does she have a comment about *Roe v. Wade?*" "Is there some particular reason she could have a comment about it today?" Martha wondered. "Yes. The decision was announced in Washington this morning at ten," the reporter replied. "How?" "She won," he said. At the same time Patty McKool, who was answering my Capitol office phones, received a call from an NBC *Today* show reporter asking for comments.

Indeed, that morning at ten the Supreme Court had announced that by a vote of seven to two the Texas anti-abortion statutes had been ruled unconstitutional as violating the constitutional right of privacy. The plaintiffs in *Doe v. Bolton* had also won most of their points, but the importance of that opinion was overshadowed by the breadth of the *Roe* decision. Supreme Court decisions set the supreme law of the land; the decisions in *Roe* and *Doe* affected the laws of every state that had provisions similar to those of Texas and Georgia. Abortion was no longer illegal.

Pandemonium broke out. The phones erupted with press calls, congratulatory calls, calls requesting information about the decision. There was mass confusion and commotion; we were transferring calls and I was running back and forth between my Capitol office and our law office at home. Ron and Martha were managing the chaos at the law office, despite the fact that his favorite uncle had just died and he had a trial scheduled a few days later. Ruth Bowers pitched in to handle the people streaming through at the Capitol: neighboring office staffs coming to see what the noise was all about, supporters joining in the celebration, and press photographers clamoring for pictures. Apparently people remembered how much I love fresh flowers: I have a mental image of bouquets filling up the reception area, of flowers everywhere. Because of the maelstrom that day, through the years I had come to remember having been at home when I first heard about the decision. But recent interviews with others have clarified for me that I first heard the news at the Capitol

Linda [Coffee] got the news on the radio while driving to work. When she arrived at her office, a senior partner told her that news about *Roe* would soon be preempted by other news: Lyndon Johnson had died. Linda called to tell me that, and to share the excitement of victory. Our conversation started on a somber note because of that famous Texan's death, but it picked up as our thoughts turned to the Supreme Court's action. We could not get over the fact that we, two young women lawyers not long out of law school, relatively inexperienced, who few people thought had a chance, had contributed to winning a crucial Supreme Court decision. It was a decision that freed women from the fear of unwanted pregnancy, a decision that freed doctors to practice medicine according to their best training, a decision we felt would result in fewer unwanted children. As we talked, however, we kept returning to questions about the content of the decision and therefore its impact, questions we couldn't answer until we knew more about the Court's specific words. . . .

I tried but was unable to reach Jane Roe. I finally gave up, thinking that since she remained anonymous she would not get caught off-guard by press calls; I assumed she had heard or would see press reports, since by then the news of the decision was being mentioned during every newscast.

John and Mary Doe had already heard when I got through to them; they had already been speaking with friends and relatives about the news. Dr. Hallford, we imagined, must be very happy now that the two indictments against him would be dropped. Dr. Hodgson certainly was. She was driving through a pouring rain on her way to Sanibel, Florida, for a vacation when the announcement came on the radio. She stopped at the next roadside phone to call home for more details and to rejoice that her medical license was now safe.

At the *Rag* office in Austin, normally intense, hardworking writers were dancing. Judy Smith was amazed. "We never thought we would accomplish the level of decision that came back. We were so naive." The wonderful part, she thought, was that women would never again know the agony she had seen others go through. She saw the decision not as something Austin volunteers had done, but as something broader: "All this energy from people all over the country had gone into it, and things were changed. That day was a celebration of the effort."...

My friend in Washington called back to describe the opinion to me; I had gotten other details from reporters who called. I began to do press interviews but was still circumspect in what I said; I wanted to *read* the opinion. My official statement was brief:

> I am pleased because of the impact this decision will have on the lives of many women who in the past have suffered because of the current Texas law. I am especially pleased that the decision is a solid seven-to-two decision, and that it was based on the right of privacy. I feel very humble to be able to represent the class of women affected by this decision and hope their lives will be better for it.

THE REACTION

Around noon I received the Supreme Court telegram: "JUDGMENT ROE AGAINST WADE TODAY AFFIRMED IN PART AND REVERSED IN PART. JUDGMENT DOE AGAINST BOLTON MODIFIED AND AFFIRMED. OPINIONS AIRMAILED." I wished I could have a copy more rapidly than that.

Texas governor Dolph Briscoe responded tersely to the decision: "I am today asking the attorney general for his evaluation of this ruling and for the alternatives open to Texas as a result of the Supreme Court's decision." Lieutenant Governor Bill

Hobby said, "It is my opinion that the best solution is one in which the state is neutral on the subject of abortion. I believe the medical profession of Texas will respond to the decision and will treat abortion as a medical matter in a responsible way."...

There were spontaneous celebrations for the Court's decision around the country. Reactions from many recognized women leaders flashed across the news wires. People often tell me that they remember vividly where they were when they heard about two events: the death of President John F. Kennedy and the decision in *Roe v. Wade*. That decision represented a change of immense proportions in the lives and futures of American women.

It wasn't until the end of the workday that Ron, Martha Davis, and I—the entire law office staff—could take a few minutes to savor the win. We shared the reactions of those we had called and those who had called us. Ron noted that the decision had been announced the first Monday after Nixon was inaugurated for his second term; that seemed to us to support the rumors that the Court had held up announcing its decision in part out of consideration for Nixon. Of Course, Martha insisted it was her typing and keeping us organized that fall that carried the day....

I could hardly believe that at twenty-seven years of age I had won an important Supreme Court case. This was, I felt, an opportunity to broaden my focus to other areas—rape-law reform, parental custody matters, the needs of children and the poor, health care, working conditions, the environment, and a long list of other concerns. I could move on. After all, I had never meant for the abortion issue to be my focus forever.

Ron and I agreed that the Court's decision was an opportunity for all women. The battle was never "for abortion"—abortion was not what we wanted to encourage. The battle was for the basic right of women to make their own decisions. There was a basic question underlying the specific issue of abortion: Who is to control and define the lives of women? And our answer was: Not the government!

Ron and I discussed our belief that the Court's decision in

Roe was a declaration for human liberty, and was faithful to the values of the nation's founders. They had created a country where the government would not be allowed to control their most private lives—not their speech, not their religion, not their domestic habits. We felt we had been true to that tradition. The "system," it seemed, did in fact work. I had always been taught to work within the system. When others had scoffed, I just kept plodding along that path—and in the end we had won a prize bigger than we ever dreamed. Our victory solidified my faith in law, the court process, and the wisdom of our nation's founders; the system they had created was resilient, and had proved its ability to adapt to changing times.

Some people learned about the decision after newspapers with front-page stories about it hit the stands. Jane Roe was quoted in *The Boston Globe* of May 15, 1989, as saying:

> [My roommate] was taking a shower while I was reading about the verdict in the living room. When she came out, I said, "What do you think of this Jane Roe?" She said, "I think she's great." I said, "Would you like to meet her?" She said, "Yeah." I stood up and said, "Hello, my name is Norma.". . .

THE OPINION

The copy of the *Roe* opinion sent by the Court arrived a few days after the decision. It was a thrill to hold the document Blackmun wrote for the Court. I skimmed it first for the main points:

• A direct appeal was proper because of the specific denial of injunctive relief regarding a statute declared unconstitutional by a three-judge federal court.

• Roe had standing to sue; the Does and Dr. Hallford did not. (Geesh, I thought, we went backward on that part. At least the lower court had recognized Hallford's standing. But it didn't matter; the outcome freed Hallford anyway.)

• The natural termination of Roe's pregnancy did not cancel her status as an appropriate plaintiff. Under strict mootness principles, hers would be a situation "capable of repetition, yet evading review."

• The Texas statute violated the due-process clause of the

Fourteenth Amendment, which protects from state action the right to privacy, including a woman's qualified right to terminate pregnancy.

• The state, however, had a legitimate interest in protecting both the pregnant woman's health and the potentiality of human life.

I settled back with my feet up to read the majority opinion in detail and savor its words. First the Court noted the sensitive nature of the subject:

> We forthwith acknowledge our awareness of the sensitive and emotional nature of the abortion controversy, of the vigorous opposing views, even among physicians, and of the deep and seemingly absolute convictions that the subject inspires. One's philosophy, one's experiences, one's exposure to the raw edges of human existence, one's religious training, one's attitudes toward life and family and their values, and the moral standards one establishes and seeks to observe, are all likely to influence and to color one's thinking and conclusions about abortion.

Blackmun then reviewed the Texas statute, the facts about the plaintiffs, and procedurally how the case had arrived at the Supreme Court. He examined the State's claims that the case was moot since Jane Roe was not pregnant when it reached the Supreme Court:

> But when, as here, pregnancy is a significant fact in the litigation, the normal 266-day human gestation period is so short that the pregnancy will come to term before the usual appellate process is complete. If that termination makes a case moot, pregnancy litigation seldom will survive much beyond the trial stage, and appellate review will be effectively denied. Our law should not be that rigid. Pregnancy often comes more than once to the same woman, and in the general population; if man is to survive, it will always be with us. Pregnancy provides a classic justification for a conclusion of nonmootness. It truly could be "capable of repetition, yet evading review."

Won that one, I thought. So the end of her pregnancy had not made the issue moot. . . .

Blackmun reexamined the reasons advanced to explain historically the enactment of criminal abortion laws and to justify their existence. First, he noted, "it has been argued occasionally that these laws were the product of a Victorian social concern to discourage illicit sexual conduct." But the State had not advanced that argument. A second reason concerned abortion as a medical procedure. However, Blackmun pointed out, abortion was no longer the very dangerous procedure it once was; appellants and various *amici,* he said, "refer to medical data indicating that abortion in early pregnancy . . . is now relatively safe." A third reason, he said, was "the State's interest—some phrase it in terms of duty—in protecting prenatal life." But here Blackmun commented that those challenging the anti-abortion statutes had "sharply disputed" that such was a reason for the statutes' being passed, and he noted a lack of any legislative history to support that argument. I had not been reading the extensive footnotes at the bottom of each page closely, but sure enough, when I did I found several referring to Cyril Means's writings; I knew he would be pleased.

The opinion got even better from my perspective when Blackmun began to write of privacy. . . .

> This right of privacy, whether it be founded in the Fourteenth Amendment's concept of personal liberty and restrictions upon state action, as we feel it is, or, as the District Court determined, in the Ninth Amendment's reservation of rights to the people, is broad enough to encompass a woman's decision whether or not to terminate her pregnancy. The detriment that the State would impose upon the pregnant woman by denying this choice altogether is apparent.

I wanted to stand and cheer!

But then came some not so good news. Blackmun noted that I had argued that the woman's right is absolute, and indicated that "with this we do not agree." Some state regulations in areas protected by the right to privacy would be appropriate,

Blackmun wrote, for reasons of safeguarding health, maintaining medical standards, and protecting what he called "potential life." "At some point in pregnancy," the opinion said, "these respective interests become sufficiently compelling to sustain regulation of the factors that govern the abortion decision." One sentence firmly stated the Court's disagreement with "the claim asserted by some *amici* that one has an unlimited right to do with one's body as one pleases.". . .

The Court did say that "regulation limiting these rights may be justified only by a 'compelling state interest'" and that "legislative enactments must be narrowly drawn to express only the legitimate state interests at stake." It seemed to be limiting the signal it was giving the states. But still I worried that the justices were underestimating the ingenuity and dogged determination of the opposition.

Next in the opinion was a lengthy section about the interest the state had advocated, that of preserving "unborn life" and explaining that the state had not treated the fetus as a person in legal ways. . . .

> throughout the major portion of the 19th century prevailing legal abortion practices were far freer than they are today, persuades us that the word "person," as used in the Fourteenth Amendment, does not include the unborn.

I remembered that night Ron had stayed up for hours writing, as I typed, the section in our brief on the beginning of legal rights. The Court apparently considered it important. Blackmun went on to write:

> Texas urges that, apart from the Fourteenth Amendment, life begins at conception and is present throughout pregnancy, and that, therefore, the State has a compelling interest in protecting that life from and after conception. We need not resolve the difficult question of when life begins. When those trained in the respective disciplines of medicine, philosophy, and theology are unable to arrive at any consensus, the judiciary, at this point in the development of man's knowledge, is not in a position to speculate as to the answer. . . .

Blackmun outlined concepts about "when life begins" that had held sway in various groups throughout history. He noted that the Roman Catholic Church had come to its current position that life begins at conception relatively recently but that it was one shared by many non-Catholics as well. However, he wrote, "substantial problems for precise definition of this view are posed . . . by new embryological data that purport to indicate that conception is a 'process' over time, rather than an event, and by new medical techniques such as menstrual extraction, the 'morning-after' pill, implantation of embryos, artificial insemination, and even artificial wombs."

To end his comments about "when life begins," Blackmun pointed out that areas of law, other than arguably criminal abortion laws, have "been reluctant to endorse any theory that life, as we recognize it, begins before live birth or to accord legal rights to the unborn except in narrowly defined situations and except when the rights are contingent upon live birth." Blackmun almost quoted from Ron's arguments when he wrote that tort law did not involve prenatal injuries and that rights of inheritance were contingent upon a live birth. He concluded simply: "In short, the unborn have never been recognized in the law as persons in the whole sense."

I checked off the significant points: There is a constitutional right of privacy; pregnancy is fundamental; the State had no compelling reason to prohibit abortion to the extent the anti-abortion laws had provided. The Texas laws were unconstitutional. . . .

The Court went on to outline a scheme for state regulation and procedures a state might implement if it chose to act . . .

(a) For the stage prior to approximately the end of the first trimester, the abortion decision and its effectuation must be left to the medical judgment of the pregnant woman's attending physician.

(b) For the stage subsequent to approximately the end of the first trimester, the State, in promoting its interest in the health of the mother, may, if it chooses, regulate the abortion procedure in ways that are reasonably related to maternal health.

(c) For the stage subsequent to viability the State, in promoting its interest in the potentiality of human life, may, if it chooses, regulate, and even proscribe, abortion except where it is necessary, in appropriate medical judgment, for the preservation of the life or health of the woman.

I considered what I had just read. Never in any of our briefs had we suggested anything about a trimester approach to pregnancy. Never in any of the State's briefs or in the amicus briefs was there anything like that. Nothing like that had been spoken of directly in oral argument. . . .

The comment that "the abortion decision . . . must be left to . . . the pregnant woman's attending physician" would also raise hackles among feminists. It seemed to take the decision from the woman and give it to her doctor. We hoped abortion would become a part of routine medical care, generally provided by a woman's regular gynecologist or obstetrician or the doctor she went to for other reasons. Of course she would seek medical advice in the event of pregnancy, but we always meant for the basic decision to remain hers. . . .

I picked up the opinion on *Doe v. Bolton.* Blackmun first set out the differences between the Texas and Georgia statutes. Then the Court basically relied on its opinion in *Roe,* but it also said explicitly that certain of what I called hurdles or roadblocks were invalid: namely, the requirement that abortions be performed in hospitals meeting standards set by the Joint Commission on Accreditation of Hospitals, approval by a hospital abortion committee, confirmation by two independent physicians, and residence . . .

OBSTACLES

That day as I read, I rejoiced that the decision was seven to two, that it was strong and clear, and that it established a fundamental right of privacy extending to the abortion issue. An important court doctrine is *stare decisis:* it is a tradition that present courts respect the decisions of the past. One of the most important functions of lawyers is to predict how a court will decide a specific issue; their tool for doing that is the body of past decisions. *Roe* would now become part of our respected body of law and established case law; future courts would be bound by its words and provisions.

Roe v. Wade became the law of the land and a national icon; the Court took no further action on pending cases. The rulings affected the laws in forty-four states, thirty-one of them with statutes similar to Georgia's. There were follow-up actions in many state legislatures and courts after the *Roe* and *Doe* decisions. In many of those states the laws were declared unconstitutional by state or federal courts or by opinion of the state attorney general. Some state legislatures immediately passed new statutes; other legislatures—as in Texas—did not pass any new regulations until years later. The pattern across the nation regarding abortion regulation was extremely varied. . . .

There was a short lull while advocates of choice celebrated the legal victory, and then attention quickly shifted to making the words a reality. The new priority was to ensure that women had access to contraception, abortion, and basic health services. Unless that happened, our victory would be hollow. In fact, even while I was finishing the court battle, the anticipation that we might win caused others to begin working on plans for providing safe, legal, affordable abortion services to women.

The first abortions were performed in doctors' offices. In Austin, the first legal abortion was done on the very day of the decision. Dr. Fred Hansen, who had become personally aware of the need for safe abortions when two of his patients died from illegal, back-alley abortions, had earlier ordered the necessary equipment, and it arrived fortuitously that morning. On the afternoon of the twenty-second, he had a call from a member of the UT nursing faculty who was leaving for New York to have an abortion. He told her she could cancel her reservations.

Quickly there were a handful of offices in Texas where, for $140 or so, a woman could obtain a legal abortion—she could even bring a friend to keep her company. Bobby Nelson, one of the law students who had helped with our research, went with a friend who was having an abortion and later wrote in

The Rag: "What a difference the [Court] . . . made with this rare human legal decision." She continued:

> Two important thoughts are with me: first, we must understand that the Supreme Court was responding not just to technical and impressive briefs or strong oral arguments on the rights of women. They were responding to the rallying of women across the nation—a rejection of women as reproductive machines and an acceptance for women as individuals capable of choice.
>
> Secondly, we must understand that the battle has only just begun. An abortion still costs $140, more than many pregnant women can afford; few doctors have the modern equipment; most will still require the consent of a husband.
>
> But we can begin with the token [knowledge] that it makes an immediate difference in the lives of many women. Now we can redirect our energies to other issues.

Expanding access to abortion did not go smoothly. Although a few doctors had the necessary equipment, most did not. For those who didn't, the only place to perform an abortion was in a hospital. Yet hospitals were very hesitant to open their operating rooms until they were sure they would not be in legal jeopardy. . . .

Frustrated over the slow pace of services in Texas, some people decided to speed things up. Ruth Bowers had been optimistic before the decision and urged that preparations be started for offering services. Dr. Alan Guttmacher, in San Antonio to give a speech and to see his protégé Dr. Paul Weinberg, commented that abortion clinics were needed; doctors' offices would never be able to meet the demands. Ruth gave $10,000 of Sears, Roebuck stock, and San Antonio Planned Parenthood, encouraged by its executive director, Myron Chrisman (a former pastor of a large Protestant congregation), decided to start a clinic. A place had been rented, but it was not completely set up when the decision was announced. Ruth bought furniture and, with two members of her household staff, got the location ready to open. The clinic eventually became independent of Planned Parenthood and was named Reproductive Health Services.

Most of the names of the doctors who bravely stepped forward are known only to their patients. In San Antonio they included Brandon Chenault and Foster Moore. Chenault experienced what many doctors went through: the management of the office building where he had his private practice said he would be evicted if he persisted in doing procedures in his office. Chenault responded by becoming a cooperating physician for the Planned Parenthood clinic, and continued his routine practice at his private office. Dr. Weinberg, a professor at the San Antonio medical school, contributed by instituting a program that trained medical students to perform abortions safely.

Access to abortion was not a local problem. On March 26, 1973, the executive director of the National Association for the Repeal of Abortion Laws issued a statement:

> A "wait and see" attitude prevailed as the health establishment looked to . . . state attorney general's office[s] and/or state courts for "clarification," and to . . . state health department[s] for guidelines. Catholic hospitals announced a refusal to perform abortions, non–Catholic hospitals reluctant to adopt new abortion policies but afraid of damage suits if they refused to do abortions, hedged and hid behind procedural delays. With the exception of Florida, the South continues to show strong resistance and little, if any, movement. Elsewhere some hospitals are beginning to perform first-trimester, in-hospital abortions, with few reportedly ambulatory procedures. A decline in the demand by out-of-state women in New York, Wisconsin, and Kansas clinics indicates that early abortions are becoming more available nationwide. . . . Most hospital abortions are occurring in larger cities. Very little is happening in smaller towns.
>
> The clinic picture is disappointing. Clinics have opened in Atlanta, St. Louis, San Francisco, Miami, Detroit, Columbus, Chicago, Boston, Milwaukee, Philadelphia, Pittsburgh and Erie, Pa. (in Erie at $260). Others are planned for Des Moines, Kansas, Houston, San Antonio and Fort Worth. But

elsewhere bureaucratic red tape and state laws (such as [those] requiring a certificate of need for setting up or adding to health facilities) are impeding the establishment of clinics. So is the difficulty of locating physicians willing to staff them.

Roe and *Doe* had obviously changed the legal battles being fought, but those battles—and our victory—would be insignificant if the decisions did not result in pregnant women having access to safe medical care. We had won Round 1, the Supreme Court decision. It was quickly apparent that Round 2 would be a battle to make abortion services available to women.

The Consequences of *Roe v. Wade* for Abortion Providers

Carole Joffe is a professor of sociology at the University of California at Davis and has done extensive research interviewing doctors who performed abortions before and after *Roe v. Wade*. The following selection comes from a number of interviews done with abortion providers in the 1970s. The physicians describe their reactions to the *Roe v. Wade* victory, but go on to explain that they faced a number of obstacles even after abortion was legalized. The Supreme Court decision did not change public opinion or, perhaps more importantly, the medical profession's opinion of abortion. In Joffe's interviews all of the doctors expressed that they felt institutional resistance immediately after *Roe v. Wade*. No additional resources were made readily available to the doctors, and the majority felt professionally ostracized, as if they sacrificed career advancement to offer women a basic human right. Joffe's interviews describe through first-hand accounts the immediate effect of *Roe v. Wade* and the hurdles that still needed to be overcome. The movement now needed to work just as hard to uphold that victory and to make abortion accessible by allotting the necessary resources and supporting the physicians who would continue to make sacrifices.

We were doing abortions that day when the news came over the radio. It was just an overwhelming feeling, I got tears in my eyes. . . . At last it was all over, finally, . . . never again the fear, the threats, the violence, [the threat of] going to prison,

Carole Joffe, *Doctors of Conscience: The Struggle to Provide Abortion Before and After* Roe v. Wade. Boston: Beacon Press, 1995. Copyright © 1995 by Carole Joffe. Reproduced by permission.

A TURNING POINT: *ROE V. WADE* AND ITS AFTERMATH • 111

the constant harassment, fear of the woman not being able to get service. It was a new day.

—David Bennett

Then there was January 22 [1973]. January 22 I was at home, in bed, with a cold. It was about ten in the morning. I was listening to the radio and I heard the Supreme Court's decision. I could not believe it! It was mind-boggling! I was thrilled. I was so excited I could hardly stay in bed with my illness. That [decision] meant several things to me, some on a very personal level. . . . It also provided an opportunity for me; we no longer had to be restricted by the cost constraints and the administrative constraints of the hospital. . . . Now I had the opportunity to set up something [freestanding clinic] which would be valuable for the community, a public service.

—Marty Kaufman

When *Roe v. Wade* came along, I was so relieved because now I could thumb my nose at anyone who gave me a hard time. I remember the president of the hospital used to say, "I wish we could get rid of those abortions, I hate those abortions."

—Morris Fischer

It was like a ton of bricks coming off my shoulders. . . . When (*Roe*) came out, I was literally walking with my feet off the ground. . . . Such a triumph had been accomplished by people I didn't even know.

—Caleb Barrington

These comments express the elation felt by virtually everyone interviewed for this book about the historic ruling of the U.S. Supreme Court on January 22, 1973, which legalized abortion. At the time of *Roe*, Doctors Bennett and Kaufman were practicing in states which had already liberalized their abortion laws. Nonetheless, for both men, this ruling was very significant. For Bennett, in particular, *Roe* served to validate his past record of extensive provision of illegal abortions. For both, moreover, the new ruling promised better quality of care. Women who had previously traveled from their own states to seek abortions in more liberal states would now presumably find abortions closer to home, with back-up care more readily available, if needed, after the abortion. Also, as Kaufman's comments suggest, the rulings of this historic day would further facilitate what was already in place in some locations—the freestanding abortion clinic as a new model of medical service delivery.

Fischer's comments convey the enormous relief felt by the many abortion providers in the pre-*Roe* period who had been practicing in the "gray area" of hospital committee-approved abortions, never sure if antiabortion colleagues or an ambitious district attorney would decide to investigate "unjustified" abortions.

In the period immediately before *Roe*, Barrington had just returned to his New England birthplace and had made the decision to start an abortion practice, even if that meant, ultimately, that he would be arrested. His euphoria was shared by the many abortion-sympathetic physicians of that period who, having witnessed the results of illegal abortion, now could reasonably assume that they would no longer have to choose between the practice of good medicine and their own personal freedom . . .

THE COSTS OF ABORTION WORK

The difficulties abortion providers would eventually face in the era of legalization were not immediately apparent to many of those interviewed. Rather, these physicians quickly saw the benefits of the new ruling with respect to women's health. Even this group—far more attuned than other physicians to abortion issues—were stunned to learn how much more illegal abortion there had been in the pre-*Roe* period than they had previously thought. As Ron Ehrlich commented, "I don't think we realized what was going on, the full impact of what was going on out there . . . because [now] in the emergency room, you could spend ten nights in a row in the E.R. and not see a pregnant woman miscarrying, and then, we saw three and four a night . . . so obviously, many of them were started." Similarly, Ken Gordon expressed his astonishment upon realizing how little experience the residents currently under his supervision had with miscarriages in the emergency room. "*Now* I know that many of those we thought were 'genuine' miscarriages really were not."

To be sure, some of those interviewed encountered institutional resistance immediately upon the passage of *Roe* and had to continue their advocacy activity. Eugene Fox, like several others, was driven to consider legal action to pressure his own hospital to conform to the new law. "In 1973, when the Supreme Court decision came down, I was no longer acting as chair of our department. We had a new younger chairman and I bulldozed him by threatening a lawsuit because he wouldn't have an abortion facility. He succumbed on that." When asked if he requested support from colleagues over this threatened lawsuit, Fox replied, "I had verbal support from several people, but they were like, 'I'll hold your coat, you get in there and fight.'"

In the mid-1970s, Morris Fischer returned from two years of practicing medicine abroad and assumed a professorship of obstetrics and gynecology in a medical school on the East Coast. "When I started work here, I started scheduling abortions. They told me, 'You are not allowed to do abortions in this institution.' I said, 'What are you talking about? This is 1975! *Roe v. Wade* was 1973!' . . . 'Well, we have a rule on our books.' 'Well, you can have a rule on your books that I am not going to stay here. You want my services, you want my talents, you say I am a big gun or something, then you have to have me as I am.' That very meeting when I spoke they put a motion up and it was ruled that I could do them up to and including twelve weeks but nothing beyond that. . . . They wanted to make it very clear that I wouldn't make the hospital into an abortion mill."

In some hospitals, even when the letter of the new law was obeyed, a combination of residual opposition to abortion and downright confusion as to how to implement this new service made the abortion highly unpleasant for the patient and the attending physician. Miriam Harkin recalled with distaste her first experience of attempting a hospital-based abortion in the immediate aftermath of *Roe*. "I can remember the first patient I took there to do a legal abortion, a day or two after *Roe v. Wade*. The good part was that she didn't have to go through this laborious approval committee. But she was sitting in the ward, waiting to have her abortion; the nurses would come to the door, peer at her, and make gestures of disapproval. . . . So the woman was waiting, I was waiting, the whole afternoon. Finally, the hospital administrator comes up and says we can't do this, the details of the law haven't been worked out. We had to go to another hospital, and I didn't get to do her until around five or six o'clock because we had been mucking around all day. What a hassle."

FREESTANDING ABORTION CLINICS

It was precisely the "hassles" that Harkin and others experienced in their hospitals that made the freestanding clinic so attractive. The excitement felt by many of those interviewed about the abortion clinic was that here, finally, abortion patients would be treated with some decency. As Harkin put it, "I felt it was so important to have special freestanding clinics, where there are caring people, not general medical people, not self-righteous people. Our Victorian morality has been antiabortion for so long, that even people—like the nurses—who are otherwise kind and caring can be so cruel in the abortion situation."

. . . The initial enthusiasm many abortion providing physicians felt about the freestanding clinic was also because of its innovative character as a health delivery model. As such, participating in the creation and refinement of this model offered to some the possibility of both a professional challenge and a means of upgrading the image of abortion. Barry Messinger reminisced about his decision to continue to be intensely involved in abortion work after *Roe*, particularly his leadership in establishing a freestanding clinic in his community: "I guess I'm a maverick. . . . I like to do things that are different. It was a new territory. . . . I had already been involved in dealing with women's reproduction in a number of different ways and here was a new way to help them. And it was a way to kind of show my more conservative colleagues that something new could be added to medicine, and it was going to work. And it was reputable and good." . . .

To be sure, each of the physicians interviewed for this study has a unique configuration of personal characteristics and career contingencies that helps explain his or her current assessment of abortion work, . . . We can find suggestions of some general dilemmas inherent in this work. A major problem of abortion work, as it has developed since 1973, is that for most practitioners there is little professional challenge in it once the basic technique of suction curettage has been mastered. It is true, as I have documented, that for some of the pioneers active in the period immediately before and after *Roe* it was an exciting time of innovation in both techniques and service delivery models. But most providers, even some of the "pioneers" I have cited, came to acknowledge the routinization of most abortion work. This routinization has contributed to abortion provision's relative lack of status in the larger medical community—and especially within the world of obstetrics and gynecology. Barry Messinger, himself one of the most influential of abortion innovators, spoke quite candidly about the limitations of abortion specialization as a career for those in academic medicine. Commenting on the period surrounding *Roe*, he said, "I knew that not very many of my academic colleagues were interested or willing to put time into doing abortions. . . . I also became aware of the fact that the technique was rapidly becoming simple and one would not be able to write a lot of papers about its complexities and its advances and permutations—things like that. So from that point of view, it's not a very intellectually challenging deal . . . and I think one would have had to be in early, like I was, to make certain contributions. And also it would help if one were kind of sociologically dedicated to the proposition that women should have this as part of their medical care. And I think that limited the kind of academic people who would be interested in it."

Judith Harmon, in speaking of the reluctance of mainstream physicians to become involved with the freestanding clinic movement—both immediately after *Roe* and in the present— gave an even more explicitly feminist twist to her analysis. "Definitely then, and even maybe more so today, the academic people saw you couldn't afford to get your hands dirty with this stuff unless you were an extremely powerful person and just happened to be enough of a humanist. . . . You know, a lower-level person couldn't possibly risk contaminating their career. . . . It is not intellectual, that's for sure. . . . I don't think it's all that different from any of the other 'women's issues,' even in ob/gyn it's not actually okay to *care* about women in that kind of way. . . . You can only care intellectually about pituitary tumors in women. . . . It's kind of like being interested in daycare or something! I think the same is true about contraception . . . things like barrier method, condoms or diaphragms, who would care about that? It's too ordinary." . . .

LEGAL YET UNACCEPTABLE

Some physicians who began doing abortions after legalization came into conflict with partners who were uneasy about such activity. Charles Swensen, a particularly visible spokesman for abortion in his state, spoke of such a conflict with his partners in a large group practice. "The senior partners were in principle supportive of abortion but they did not like the notoriety that I as an individual was receiving in the press, and as a result they docked my income by about 15 percent. . . . We had a meeting and they said, 'Okay, we've calculated this, and this is where we are setting your percentage of remuneration that will come for the next four years.' I said, 'What can I do to improve that for the next go-around?' and they said, 'Well, you should get out of the abortion business.'"

But if practitioners who combined abortion work with other activities suffered a certain chilly reception from colleagues, the ostracism felt by those who chose full-time abortion work is even more evident. David Bennett spoke with bitterness about the difficult relations he had with various sectors of the medical community in the period immediately after *Roe.* In attempting to establish a nonprofit abortion clinic and get local physicians who would both serve on the board and perform abortions, Bennett found that his history as a provider of illegal abortion tainted his image among his would-be colleagues. "There were some who said they'd be willing to provide abortion service with such a set-up but they didn't want to have anything to do with me.... It was because I was an 'abortionist.'... An abortionist is a despicable person. They assumed you did it for the money, you didn't have the qualifications to be a real doctor ... you were either a drug addict, an alcoholic, a ne'er do well, you couldn't maintain a practice or you were owned by the Mafia.... You weren't a good person and probably weren't a good doctor either. At the very least, you were an embarrassment to the medical community."

CHAPTER 4

ABORTION IN THE TWENTY-FIRST CENTURY

AMERICAN
SOCIAL
MOVEMENTS

The Abortion Rights Movement Must Broaden Its Focus to Stay Viable

MARLENE GERBER FRIED

Marlene Gerber Fried is a professor in the Civil Liberties and Public Policy Program at Hampshire College, in Amherst, Massachusetts, and also serves as cochair of the National Network of Abortion Funds, a group which helps women pay for and travel to the United States for safe abortions. In the following selection, taken from *From Abortion to Reproductive Freedom: Transforming a Movement*, Fried argues that the abortion rights movement faltered and became essentially nonexistent after abortion was legalized in 1974. She goes on to say that it was not until 1977 and the passage of the Hyde Amendment, which prohibited Medicaid funding of abortion, that the movement began to be reenergized. However, in 1989, when the Supreme Court decision in *Webster v. Reproductive Health Service* cut off access to public funding by prohibiting abortions in public facilities and in private hospitals that received public funds, the movement faltered. Although the Hyde Amendment and *Webster* proved to be huge setbacks for the movement, the legislation did not destroy the movement nor its work to keep abortion legal.

Nevertheless, Fried argues that the structure and tactics of the movement changed; in the face of a growing countermovement, the movement became defensive rather than offensive. Fried theorizes that in order for the movement to remain viable it is essential to link the abortion rights movement to other reproductive rights issues. Furthermore, she suggests that activists must be aggressive and must choose leaders who

Marlene Gerber Fried, *From Abortion to Reproductive Freedom: Transforming a Movement*. Boston: South End Press, 1990. Copyright © 1990 by South End Press. Reproduced by permission.

will remain aggressive. Most importantly, Fried suggests, is the need for activists within the movement to engage in dialogue with each other so as to progress the movement farther than ever before.

POLITICS OF THE PRO-CHOICE MOVEMENT: ON THE DEFENSIVE

The abortion rights movement essentially folded after abortion became legal. While more radical segments of the movement mobilized in 1977 after the Hyde Amendment prohibited federal Medicaid funding of abortion, it was not until the threat of a constitutional amendment that would ban all U.S. abortions was posed in 1981 that a visible mainstream abortion rights movement re-emerged.

The 1980s movement formed as a reaction to the backlash, and was shaped by the need to respond to an all-out anti-choice campaign, one with initiatives in legislatures, in the courts, and in the streets. In an effort to hold the line, the new abortion rights movement rarely dared talk about abortion or women's rights, preferring instead to focus on the intolerance and extremism of the other side. The pro-choice movement attempted to sanitize its own demands. Insisting on abortion rights as a necessary condition of all women's sexual freedom continues to be seen as too threatening, too risky, too selfish. Instead, the movement turned to the more innocuous and ambiguous language of "choice" and "personal freedom." The women's movement fought to bring women's reproductive lives out of the private sphere, arguing that our personal choices were political. How ironic that the pro-choice movement now argues that abortion is private and personal, not political.

In trying to hold onto past gains, the pro-choice movement has failed to pursue new ones, either by solidifying its own membership or speaking out to the public. *Roe v. Wade* was not the first step of a feminist agenda for reproductive control; it turned out to be the *only* step, defended by appeals to the right to privacy—the importance of keeping the government out of our personal lives—and to religious tolerance.

Those activists who have argued for a radical reproductive

rights approach have had to struggle simply to put abortion and women's lives back into the debate. There seems to be no place at all in the ideology of "choice" for public discussion of women's needs for autonomy and sexual freedom and for the societal changes that would make these possible.

This defensive posture is problematic in many ways. While the pro-choice movement must respond to the attacks on abortion and does not control the timing or place of the attacks, it *can* control the terms of the response. . . .

POLITICAL IMPLICATIONS: TRANSFORMING THE MOVEMENT

Can we defend abortion rights without becoming a defensive movement—one that settles for less out of fear of losing more? Can we go from a movement focused primarily on the narrow right of legal abortion to a movement for reproductive freedom? Can we become an inclusive movement whose politics and leadership reflect the diversity of women's lives and needs?

The current political scene provides many opportunities for the pro-choice movement to link abortion to other reproductive rights issues. The attack on abortion is part of a larger attack on sexual freedom. The effort to curtail abortion rights, like the effort to manipulate fears about AIDS, is an attempt to suppress sexual freedom. The *Webster* decision links defense of abortion rights to defense of public health care and facilities and to the struggle for economic justice. As in the *McRae* case (1981, the Supreme Court upheld the Hyde Amendment) the Court has made painfully obvious that poor women will bear the brunt of erosions in abortion rights. In the past, however, the pro-choice movement has failed to connect the defense of abortion rights to the struggle for better health care and economic conditions of poor women and women of color. Is it possible now to orient the politics of the pro-choice movement in this direction? I think so.

Women of color, poor women, gay men and lesbians, union activists, and civil rights activists have all participated in the struggle for reproductive rights. The amicus brief for *Webster* had broad support from groups representing many diverse constituencies.

In April 1989, a group of about 150 grassroots activists from all over the country, a majority of whom were women of color, came to a conference in Washington, D.C. called "In Defense of Roe." The messages from that meeting were significant and clear: women of color are participating in the struggle for reproductive rights; women of color are prepared to take the leadership in the struggle for abortion rights so long as that struggle is not separated from other aspects of reproductive freedom. The struggle must be seen to be about women's survival in all of its breadth.

This means having a wider vision of women's reproductive, social, and economic needs, reflecting that vision in policies and practices, and sharing financial and organizational resources. We must also challenge our assumptions about who is and can be active around reproductive rights. For white women, this implies challenging a self-image as "the leaders" in the movement. As currently organized, the movement does not speak for all women nor does its leadership reflect broader commitments.

The abortion rights movement is coming together in an effort to re focus the debate so that women's lives become the central issue. In doing so, more radical demands are emerging. Women are calling for not only the right to choose among existing options, but are questioning why they lack the power to create the options themselves. There is a re-awakening of interest in women-controlled health care and abortion. There is a call for women to control the development and distribution of abortifacient drugs like RU-486. Women are saying they will take on the task of keeping the clinics open regardless of the legal status of abortion. Millions of women seem prepared not only to have abortions even if abortion is criminalized, but to publicly announce their intentions to do so.

Civil disobedience and other forms of direct action are being widely discussed. The refusal to allow abortion to go underground in the way that it was pre-*Roe* is striking. The women's movement has permanently changed the consciousness of many women. Young women feel entitled to abortion rights, birth control, jobs, and other aspects of equality. And now they seem prepared to fight to secure these rights.

This is a time for our movement to be aggressive. On this and other political and strategic questions, the issue of leadership is a crucial one. While mainstream groups are somewhat divided on all of these points, their membership and leadership remain predominantly white and middle-class. This is also true of more radical, local, grassroots reproductive rights groups and left-wing groups active on the issue. While it may be tempting to move at once to rebuild national Left-feminist networks, which were dominated by white women, these efforts will fail if they do not insure women of color equal partnership in the movement.

Reproductive rights activists need to engage in a dialogue so we can set a post-*Webster* agenda to take us beyond where we have ever been. The need to deepen understandings of choice and reproductive rights is as acute within the pro-choice movement as outside of it. Political development has been one of the casualties of the need to constantly defend the bottom line. We have seen the fragility not only of our court-granted rights, but of public consciousness. Even as prochoice electoral support is booming, the climate is shaky because it is taken as a given that abortion is a necessary *evil*, morally problematic, something to be avoided. This way of thinking is common not just among our enemies, but also among our friends. . . .

Grassroots activists can take heart from the emergent radical tendencies and re-focus the struggle for abortion rights on women's lives and needs, incorporating a broad definition of what it takes for all women to be able to make uncoerced reproductive decisions. The abortion rights movement will grow stronger through this effort. And in this process, the women's movement as a whole will become a more unified, powerful force for all women's liberation.

Legal, Safe Abortions Remain Threatened

BELL HOOKS

In the following excerpt bell hooks writes of the class and race components of the history of the abortion movement as well as her hopes for the future of the movement. Hooks speaks of the abortion rights movement's success in helping to get affordable, accessible, risk-free contraceptives to women and in keeping abortion legal. However, she argues that these successes essentially created the demise of the organized abortion rights movement. She contends that the movement's demise has caused the stability of woman's rights to falter, and now women find themselves bracing for another battle to retain the right to control their reproductive rights. The focus of hooks's argument is that without the right to safe and inexpensive abortions, women lose all control over their bodies. She argues that women of all races and classes must continue to work *together* to fight against such a looming injustice. In her opinion, so as to not lose ground on issues of supreme importance to women and to preserve women's freedom, the feminist movement needs to be, and can be, revitalized through activist cooperation.

When contemporary feminist movement began the issues that were projected as most relevant were those that were directly linked to the experiences of highly educated white women (most of whom were materially privileged.) Since feminist movement followed in the wake of civil rights and sexual liberation it seemed appropriate at the time that issues around the female body were foregrounded. Contrary to the image the mass media presented to the world, a feminist movement starting with women burning bras at a Miss Amer-

bell hooks, *Feminism Is for Everybody: Passionate Politics*. Boston: South End Press, 2000. Copyright © 2000 by Gloria Watkins. Reproduced by permission of Pluto Press and in the United States and Canada by South End Press.

ica pageant then later images of women seeking abortions, one of the first issues which served as a catalyst for the formation of the movement was sexuality—the issue being the rights of women to choose when and with whom they would be sexual. The sexual exploitation of women's bodies had been a common occurrence in radical movements for social justice whether socialist, civil rights, etc.

When the so-called sexual revolution was at its peak the issue of free love (which usually meant having as much sex with whomever one desired) brought females face to face with the issue of unwanted pregnancy. Before there could be any gender equity around the issue of free love women needed access to safe, effective contraceptives and abortions. While individual white women with class privilege often had access to both these safeguards, most women did not. Often individual women with class privilege were too ashamed of unwanted pregnancy to make use of their more direct access to responsible health care. The women of the late '60s and early '70s who clamored for abortions had seen the tragedies of illegal abortions, the misery of forced marriages as a consequence of unwanted pregnancies. Many of us were the unplanned children of talented, creative women whose lives had been changed by unplanned and unwanted pregnancies; we witnessed their bitterness, their rage, their disappointment with their lot in life. And we were clear that there could be no genuine sexual liberation for women and men without better, safer contraceptives—without the right to a safe, legal abortion. . . .

TAKING A RISK: DAMAGING SEXUAL LIBERATION

The development of effective though not totally safe birth control pills (created by male scientists most of whom were not anti-sexist) truly paved the way for female sexual liberation more so than abortion rights. Women like myself who were in our late teens when the pill was first widely available were spared the fear and shame of unwanted pregnancies. Responsible birth control liberated many women like myself who were pro-choice but not necessarily pro-abortion for ourselves from having to personally confront the issue. While I never had an unwanted pregnancy in the heyday of sexual liberation, many of my peers saw abortion as a better choice than conscious, vigilant use of birth control pills. And they did frequently use abortion as a means of birth control. Using the pill meant a woman was directly confronting her choice to be sexually active. Women who were more conscientious about birth control were often regarded as sexually loose by men. It was easier for some females just to let things happen sexually then take care of the "problem" later with abortions. We now know that both repeated abortions or prolonged use of birth control pills with high levels of estrogen were not risk-free. Yet women were willing to take risks to have sexual freedom—to have the right to choose.

The abortion issue captured the attention of mass media because it really challenged the fundamentalist thinking of Christianity. It directly challenged the notion that a woman's reason for existence was to bear children. It called the nation's attention to the female body as no other issue could have done. It was a direct challenge to the church. Later all the other reproductive issues that feminist thinkers called attention to were often ignored by mass media. The long-range medical problems from cesareans and hysterectomies were not juicy subjects for mass media; they actually called attention to a capitalist patriarchal male-dominated medical system that controlled women's bodies and did with them anything they wanted to do. To focus on gender injustice in these arenas would have been too radical for a mass media which remains deeply conservative and for the most part anti-feminist.

THE STRUGGLE CONTINUES
No feminist activists in the late '60s and early '70s imagined that we would have to wage a battle for women's reproductive rights in the '90s. Once feminist movement created the cultural revolution which made the use of relatively risk-free contraceptives acceptable and the right to have a safe, legal abortion pos-

sible women simply assumed those rights would no longer be questioned. The demise of an organized, radical feminist mass-based political movement coupled with anti-feminist backlash from an organized right-wing political front which relies on fundamentalist interpretations of religion placed abortion back on the political agenda. The right of females to choose is now called into question.

Sadly the anti-abortion platform has most viciously targeted state-funded, inexpensive, and, when need be, free abortions. As a consequence women of all races who have class privilege continue to have access to safe abortions—continue to have the right to choose—while materially disadvantaged women suffer. Masses of poor and working-class women lose access to abortion when there is no government funding available for reproductive rights health care. Women with class privilege do not feel threatened when abortions can be had only if one has lots of money because they can still have them. But masses of women do not have class power. More women than ever before are entering the ranks of the poor and indigent. Without the right to safe, inexpensive, and free abortions they lose all control over their bodies. If we return to a world where abortions are only accessible to those females with lots of money we risk the return of public policy that will aim to make abortion illegal. It's already happening in many conservative states. Women of all classes must continue to make abortions safe, legal, and affordable. . . .

RENEWED FERVOR

As we seek to rekindle the flames of mass-based feminist movement reproductive rights will remain a central feminist agenda. If women do not have the right to choose what happens to our bodies we risk relinquishing rights in all other areas of our lives. In renewed feminist movement the overall issue of reproductive rights will take precedence over any single issue. This does not mean that the push for legal, safe, inexpensive abortions will not remain central, it will simply not be the only issue that is centralized. If sex education, preventive health care, and easy access contraceptives are offered every female, fewer of us will have unwanted pregnancies. As a consequence the need for abortions would diminish.

Losing ground on the issue of legal, safe, inexpensive abortion means that women lose ground on all reproductive issues. The anti-choice movement is fundamentally anti-feminist. While it [is] possible for women to individually choose never [to] have an abortion, allegiance to feminist politics means that they still are pro-choice, that they support the right of females who need abortions to choose whether or not to have them. Young females who have always had access to effective contraception—who have never witnessed the tragedies caused by illegal abortions—have no firsthand experience of the powerlessness and vulnerability to exploitation that will always be the outcome if females do not have reproductive rights. Ongoing discussion about the wide range of issues that come under the heading of reproductive rights is needed if females of all ages and our male allies in struggle are to understand why these rights are important. This understanding is the basis of our commitment to keeping reproductive rights a reality for all females. Feminist focus on reproductive rights is needed to protect and sustain our freedom.

March with Us

ANTHONY ROMERO

On April 24, 2004, over 1 million individuals gathered in Washington, D.C., to voice opposition to government attacks on women's reproductive rights and health. It was a march of historical proportion. The American Civil Liberties Union, Black Women's Health Imperative, Feminist Majority, NARAL Pro-Choice America, National Latina Institute for Reproductive Health, National Organization of Women, and Planned Parenthood Federation of America organized the march. Participants gathered to walk to ensure that all women have the right to choose whether to have children, that contraceptives and abortion services remain available and accessible, and that the fundamental right of women to control their lives is upheld. The March for Women's Lives hosted a number of speakers, one of which was Anthony Romero of the American Civil Liberties Union. The following selection is Romero's speech, in which he inspires marchers to promote issues of choice, justice, and freedom. He inspires all to march, to fight, and to continue fighting because women can and will retain their civil rights.

W elcome my friends.

The American Civil Liberties Union is proud to join you today as we stand together in the name of reproductive freedom for all.

As a democratic and free nation, we are at a critical moment in our history. In recent years we have witnessed an unequalled attack on our civil liberties, and the right to reproductive freedom has been a prime target. We are here today to demand an end to the government's incursion into our personal lives and to stop the political assault on reproductive rights.

The government does not belong in our bedrooms. It does

Pro-choice supporters rally and march in Washington, D.C., to raise awareness and advocate for women's civil rights.

not belong in our doctors' offices. It does not belong in the bank accounts of innocent Americans, and should not have the power to monitor their e-mail, or track their bookstore purchases, or scrutinize the books they check out of local libraries. Our fundamental right to privacy is under serious attack by this government.

The decision of whether or not to have a child is among the most private decisions a person can make. This is true no matter who you are or where you live. And yet, our government continues to enact laws and polices that deny this basic human right. The assault on reproductive freedom must end now.

I was a young boy when I first heard the whispered stories of a beloved family member's self-induced abortion. She had had four children and worked long hours in a nearby factory to support them. One day, she found herself pregnant again. She couldn't even begin to imagine how she could provide for another child. But this was decades before the U.S. Supreme Court declared a woman's fundamental right to reproductive freedom.

Desperate to end the pregnancy, she took an extreme measure that put her own life at risk. Thankfully, she was one of the lucky ones. She lived to speak about her experience. But her health bore the scars of this tragic event until the day she died.

The policies of the current administration threaten to make this story the story of future generations of American women. Anti-choice forces currently control the White House. They control both houses of Congress. And they control many state legislatures. Our opponents are more determined than ever to undermine women's autonomy and extend the government's reach into our private lives. We say today that the assault on reproductive freedom must end now.

Women of color, poor women, young women, and women living in rural areas have been hardest hit by the war on reproductive rights. Already, because of the policies and laws passed since our last march, the ability to obtain basic reproductive health care has all but vanished for too many women.

Reproductive freedom means not only access to safe and legal abortion. It means access to contraceptives, access to prenatal care, access to treatment for sexually transmitted diseases, and access to accurate sexuality education.

The ACLU is marching to stop government-imposed roadblocks to basic health care. Thousands of card-carrying members are here today to ensure that all women—regardless of race, age, ethnicity, or income—have access to the full range of reproductive health services. We march so that all women will live in a world in which they can make decisions—free from government interference—about their own health care and private reproductive lives.

Growing up, I often heard my grandmother use her favorite saying from her native Puerto Rico: *"Dime con quién andas, y te diré quién eres."* (Tell me who you walk with and I will tell you who you are.")

Today, we walk among an enormous crowd of friends. Hundreds of thousands of pro-choice supporters, including thousands of ACLU members and allies, are here today to send John Ashcroft and President [George W.] Bush a message: Women's private decisions are none of your business. But our voices must be even stronger. When you return to Nebraska, California, Maine, Illinois, Louisiana, Puerto Rico, the Carolinas, take our message to your friends, family members, colleagues.

Tell them: If you believe that every woman, regardless of her economic status, should have access to birth control, walk with us.

If you believe that prenatal care must be extended to all women, walk with us.

If you believe that all women and men must have access to the full range of reproductive health services, walk with us.

If you believe that politicians should stay out of our bedrooms and out of our doctors' offices, walk with us.

If you believe that reproductive freedom is a basic human right, walk with us.

March with us. Fight with us. And keep on fighting. Thank you for being here.

Fighting the Government's Antiwoman Campaign

NANCY NORTHUP

The following selection is a statement made by Nancy Northup, president of the Center for Reproductive Rights, released the day after the 2004 U.S. presidential elections and the reelection of George W. Bush. The Center for Reproductive Rights is an organization whose mission is to use the law to advance reproductive freedom as a fundamental right that all governments are obligated to protect, respect, and fulfill. Northup's message highlights the Center for Reproductive Rights' plan of action to fight Bush's "War on Women."

During the first four years of Bush's presidency, the pro-choice movement was forced to increase its resolve and combat antiwoman, antifeminist, and antiabortion policies. The 2004 presidential election was one of extreme importance to the pro-choice movement; it was feared that the reelection of Bush meant the continued chipping away at woman's rights. The Center for Reproductive Rights fears that Bush will appoint up to three new Supreme Court judges who share the pro-life ideologies of Justices Antonin Scalia and Clarence Thomas and, in the end, overturn *Roe v. Wade.* They fear he is going to continue creating legislation such as the Partial Birth Abortion Ban Act of 2003 and continue to file briefs in the Supreme Court promoting a reversal of *Roe* in any and all cases involving abortion. Nancy Northup and the Center for Reproductive Rights are alarmed not only by the potential of Bush to overturn the legislation of *Roe v. Wade* and restrict access to safe abortions, but also by the far greater

Nancy Northup, "Responding to the Challenge of Four More Years of the Bush Administration's War on Women," www.crlp.org, November 3, 2004. Copyright © 2004 by the Center for Reproductive Rights. Reproduced by permission.

134 • THE ABORTION RIGHTS MOVEMENT

chance that Bush will continue to restrict free speech and one's ability to voice an opinion on abortion.

President Bush's reelection presents pro-choice forces with another four years of his administration's relentless war on women. The Center for Reproductive Rights is ready to continue opposing and countering every administration assault. We are confident that we will prevail because we have the strongest weapon on our side: the U.S. Constitution.

This administration has thumbed its nose at the Constitution time and time again. In its policies and practices, it has not only violated the constitutional and human rights of countless women at home and abroad, it has also endangered their health and lives. It has deprived women of access to contraception, championed the first-ever federal abortion ban, and appointed judges outspoken in their opposition to women's right to abortion. We have no doubt that the president and his administration will now step up their assaults on reproductive rights. We expect a flurry of bills to be pushed through Congress, with the president's blessing, in an attempt to chip away at *Roe v. Wade*. In both federal and state courts, we expect that legal challenges to existing laws protecting the principles of *Roe* will increase in intensity. And we expect the president to move quickly to replace any retiring Supreme Court justices with ideological clones of the two justices he most admires, Antonin Scalia and Clarence Thomas, both outspokenly anti-choice.

As we have done for the past four years, the Center for Reproductive Rights will put all of our resources into this all-important challenge to every woman's right to choose. This is not a new battle for us. We have been fighting restrictive laws that penalize low-income women, young women, and their families since 1992—and have won many times, including two landmark Supreme Court decisions. We have gone to court successfully against bans on abortion in 14 states, and most recently won a district court ruling against the federal abortion ban. The experience and expertise we have gained in litigating these cases have prepared us well for resisting new assaults on reproductive rights.

Our Plan:

- We will work to defeat any Supreme Court nominee who is hostile to *Roe v. Wade*. The Court is one to two votes away from overturning *Roe*, and we are committed to making sure this does not happen.
- We will challenge any laws that deprive teens of the right to confidential reproductive health services, including the Child Custody Protection Act, which prevents responsible adults from accompanying teens across state lines to obtain abortions.
- We will challenge the Food and Drug Administration's denial of over-the-counter status to emergency contraception. Every woman should have access to this safe method of contraception without needing a prescription.
- We will protect women from receiving false information about reproductive health services from phony providers or through biased, state-mandated materials.
- We will challenge any laws that prevent women from choosing the safest method of abortion, including state and federal abortion bans that make no exception for a woman's health.
- We will challenge restrictions on free speech, including instances where states discriminate by approving "pro-life" but not "pro-choice" license plates.
- We will challenge laws that force teens or their doctors to inform or obtain the consent of parents for abortion.
- We will challenge state laws that deny funding for abortions to low-income women who rely on Medicaid for their health care.
- We will challenge laws that regulate the practices of abortion providers or limit access to their clinics.
- We will provide resources and legal analysis to state advocates and legislators fighting to resist bills that weaken a woman's right to choose or promote bills that strengthen it.
- We will support all efforts by federal legislators to repeal the global gag rule, restore funding to UNFPA [United

Nations Population Fund], and stop reserving one-third of U.S. foreign assistance funds for HIV/AIDS prevention programs that focus upon abstinence-only education.

- We will work at the United Nations to preserve and uphold the international consensus supporting women's most basic reproductive rights.

The Abortion Rights Movement Will Remain Vital

GLORIA FELDT, WITH CAROL TRICKET JENNINGS

In *Behind Every Choice Is a Story*, Gloria Feldt, president of the Planned Parenthood Federation of America, lends her voice to the history and future of the abortion rights movement. She integrates her personal experience as an advocate and key player in the movement from 1974 to the present. In describing the current state of social and political affairs, she argues that both the movement and American society may lose ground on key issues regarding reproductive rights. However, in her opinion the movement also has the potential to create greater positive social change than it ever has before. Abortion rights organizations must mobilize and fight with optimism, spreading their vision of greater humanity, Feldt believes. She contends that although the movement faces strong, unwavering foes, the belief that women's reproductive rights are fundamental human rights will prevail and lead to the unequivocal success of the movement.

When I think about the history of our movement, I am struck not by the obstacles in our path today but by how far we have come since our beginnings. Our resolve has remained constant, but the stakes are so much higher, so our responsibilities have escalated. A movement or an organization that fails to evolve will wither and die. That's why we are looking ahead and defining the future. And that's why, having now built practical systems and the forward-looking agenda to support a growing group of activists, this movement is ready to

Gloria Feldt, with Carol Tricket Jennings, *Behind Every Choice Is a Story*. Denton: University of North Texas Press, 2002. Copyright © 2002 by the Planned Parenthood Federation of America. Reproduced by permission.

soar. And it is about time. Let us be clear about what's at stake. My right to choose abortion is equal to your right to use birth control is equal to your neighbor's right to have a child, and none of it should be decided by anyone except ourselves.

THE THREATS THAT WE FACE

Roe v. Wade is at great risk. And the same legal theory that underlies *Roe* is also the basis for the Supreme Court's landmark *Griswold v. Connecticut* decision in 1965. That decision made birth control legal for married people, nullifying the Comstock laws under which Margaret Sanger was prosecuted for distributing information about contraception and articulating a right to privacy in childbearing decisions. In between came *Eisenstadt v. Baird*, establishing that "If the right of privacy means anything, it is the right of individuals, married or single, to be free from unwarranted government intrusion into matters so fundamentally affecting a person as the decision whether to bear or beget a child."

So it is not a stretch to say that if abortion rights go, birth control rights are equally at risk. Both are built upon the same legal principle of reproductive privacy. Both could revert to being at the whim of legislative bodies. In fact, many states have never repealed their old, pre-*Roe* and *Griswold* laws.

But this time it would be much worse than in the days before 1973, when the states weighed in with their restrictions but the federal government largely kept out of it. Congress is in the act now. And the political machinery of the anti-choice groups is well oiled and ready to take advantage of any opportunity.

Further, we face adversaries who are smart, well funded, and zealously determined to prevail. They have a friend in the White House who has put his friends in charge of the Department of Justice and the Department of Health and Human Services' octopus-like tentacles reaching into a myriad of health and education offices that touch every American's life.

Since his first day in office, President George W. Bush and his appointees, alongside the anti-choice members of Congress, and aided and abetted by the now inside groups of the anti-choice far right, have been on a mission to undermine decades of progress and to roll back the reproductive rights of women here in the U.S. and around the globe. I would call their alliance the "axis of anti-choice evil." But an axis only connects its elements. The overt and covert actions of the anti-choice policymakers today are weaving a pernicious web of anti-choice evil. The individual strands might look fragile, but woven together, will soon ensnare and strangle the basic human right to freedom of childbearing choice if we do not rip them away swiftly and surely . . .

AN AGENDA FOR THE TWENTY-FIRST CENTURY

The twentieth century brought a sea change in women's lives, thanks to the many leaders and ordinary citizens who changed laws, devised better technology, and created a service network. Now, the great challenge of the twenty-first century is to elevate women's reproductive self-determination to the same level as other cherished, fundamental human and civil rights, and to make access to reproductive health and education services universal in the U.S. and globally.

To do so, we must advance an affirmative agenda—a spectacular offensive—to achieve our victories, to fight on the battlefields where we define the terms of engagement, to give prochoice constituents something to aspire to as well as something to fear, to keep the movement moving forward, in order to fulfill our commitment to make *every* child a wanted child and every woman free to define her own life.

We must deliver our visionary message about what the world will look like when our positive agenda is fulfilled, providing nothing less than hope for humanity: the freedom to dream, to make choices, and to live in peace with our planet. Every prochoice person must consider it his or her responsibility to speak up and out to deliver that message, for a movement is only as strong as the will of its individual members.

We must use the best technology to organize the American majority who support this cause and to engage them in the democratic process. We must especially educate and mentor and connect to this movement each new generation who risks taking reproductive freedom for granted and who has the most at stake if it is lost.

We must leverage our commitment to diversity to make common cause with other groups who have also been marginalized, so that we may capitalize on our collective power and influence for the common good. For we understand that embracing the rich diversity of humanity is a necessary condition to achieving the social justice and equality we seek for women.

We must make sex a good word. We must engender healthier, more realistic attitudes about sexuality in our culture in order to reduce our dismal rates of unintended pregnancy, teen pregnancy, and sexually transmitted infections.

We must control the means of producing and distributing our messages, our materials, and the outstanding reproductive health and sexuality education programming that is so often censored today. Simultaneously we must challenge the mass media to be more responsible about the images it portrays and to break down its barriers to contraceptive advertising.

Abortion must be put back where it belongs in the core of women's health care.

The fundamental right to make our own childbearing choices must be guaranteed by the U.S. Constitution and state and federal laws.

New technologies like mifepristone and emergency contraception must be supported and brought into the health care system without barriers. There is the promise of new fertility treatments to help couples trying to conceive, and a vast need to increase research funding for new contraceptives. Reproductive options are multiplying and becoming more complex, so we must lead the public debate through the ethical ramifications as well as the medical ones in a principled, not a polarized, way.

Ominous and powerful forces are arrayed against the laws and services that [make abortion available]. The biggest challenge by far is that the majority of Americans cannot believe this fact— yet. So our movement's political entities must aggressively connect the dots between public opinion and citizen behavior to deliver the pro-choice votes that support pro-choice politicians and defeat anti-choice politicians.

We must create a social climate in which policymakers of all parties find it in their best interest to support family planning, medically accurate and comprehensive sex education, and abortion rights without weaseling or waffling.

We must build the most formidable activist base anywhere. Too many pro-choice voters still simply cannot imagine that choice could disappear—so they think they need not make it a deciding factor in how they vote. "It's not an issue," I hear over and over, "We've already won." Then there is sheer denial: "They couldn't really take us backward." And an entire generation has grown up having no experience of life without choice—just as we'd hoped they would.

Well, start imagining. It *is* an issue. Choice *can* disappear. You'd better believe it can. And there's so much more we need to do to guarantee access to the full range of reproductive and sexual health care to all.

ABORTION RIGHTS ARE STILL AN ISSUE

For as long as there are unintended pregnancies, as long as there is HIV/AIDS, as long as pregnancy sentences teens to poverty and dependency, reproductive choice is an issue. Until no person can hope to be appointed to the U.S. Supreme Court or any court unless he or she expresses firm support of the human and civil right to reproductive self-determination, it is an issue. Until every human on the face of the earth has the information needed to make responsible choices about sex, pregnancy, and childbearing, until no woman dies from unsafe abortion or too many pregnancies in this world, until all pregnancies are the result of love and planning, until every child is wanted and loved, until we can all call ourselves free, it is an issue.

And once we've achieved all that—another generation will be born, and we'll start all over to ensure they have the same future. The minute we sit back and say we've won, the momentum and the moment whistle by us.

WE *MUST* CONTINUE ON

I have been there and I have done that. And I am determined it will not happen again. I am joined in this conviction by my extraordinary, courageous, strong, persistent, and increasingly energized colleagues in this movement. We have been through the crucible. We have honed our skills and our convictions. We are fierce and fearless. We are prepared to change the social climate once and for all to one that is actively supportive of reproductive rights and health care.

FOR FURTHER RESEARCH

Books

Randy Alcorn, *Prolife Answers to Prochoice Arguments.* Sisters, OR: Multnomah, 2000.

Robert M. Baird and Stuart E. Rosenbaum, eds., *The Ethics of Abortion: Pro-Life vs. Pro-Choice.* Amherst, NY: Prometheus, 2001.

Linda J. Beckman and S. Marie Harvey, eds., *The New Civil War: The Psychology, Culture, and Politics of Abortion.* Washington, DC: American Psychological Association, 1998.

Dallas A. Blanchard, *The Anti-Abortion Movement and the Rise of the Religious Right: From Polite to Fiery Protest.* New York: Twayne, 1994.

Dallas A. Blanchard, *The Anti-Abortion Movement: References and Resources.* London: G.K. Hall, 1996.

James F. Bohan, *The House of Atreus: Abortion as a Human Rights Issue.* Westport, CT: Praeger, 1999.

Leslie Bonavoglia, ed., *The Choices We Made: Twenty-Five Women and Men Speak Out About Abortion.* New York: Four Walls Eight Windows, 2001.

David Boonin, *A Defense of Abortion.* New York: Cambridge University Press, 2003.

Mary Boyle, *Rethinking Abortion: Psychology, Gender, Power, and the Law.* New York: Routledge, 1997.

Leslie Cannold, *The Abortion Myth: Feminism, Morality, and the Hard Choices Women Make.* Middleton, CT: Wesleyan University Press, 2001.

Kimberly J. Cook, *Divided Passions: Public Opinions on Abortion and the Death Penalty.* Boston: Northeastern University Press, 2001.

C.T. Coyle, *Men and Abortion: A Path to Healing.* Lewiston, NY: Life Cycle Books, 1999.

Susan E. Davis, ed., *Women Under Attack: Victories, Backlash, and the Fight for Reproductive Freedom.* Boston: South End Press, 1988.

Gloria Feldt, with Laura Fraser, *The War on Choice: The Right-Wing Attack on Women's Rights and How to Fight Back.* New York: Bantam Books, 2004.

Colin Francome, *Abortion in the USA and UK.* Burlington, VT: Ashgate, 2004.

David J. Garrow, *Liberty and Sexuality: The Right to Privacy and the Making of Roe v. Wade.* Berkeley: University of California Press, 1998.

Faye D. Ginsburg, *Contest Lives: The Abortion Debate in an American Community.* Berkeley: University of California Press, 1998.

Cynthia Gorney, *Articles of Faith: A Frontline History of the Abortion Wars.* New York: Simon and Schuster, 1998.

Mark A. Graber, *Rethinking Abortion: Equal Choice, the Constitution, and Reproductive Politics.* Princeton, NJ: Princeton University Press, 1996.

George Grant, *Grand Illusions: The Legacy of Planned Parenthood.* Nashville: Cumberland House, 2000.

N.E.H. Hull and Peter Charles Hoffer, *Roe v. Wade: The Abortion Rights Controversy in American History.* Lawrence: University Press of Kansas, 2001.

N.E.H. Hull, William James Hoffer, and Peter Charles Hoffer, eds., *The Abortion Rights Controversy in America: A Legal*

Reader. Chapel Hill: University of North Carolina Press, 2004.

Kerry N. Jacoby, *Souls, Bodies, Spirits: The Drive to Abolish Abortion Since 1973.* Westport, CT: Praeger, 1998.

Ted G. Jelen, ed., *Perspectives on the Politics of Abortion.* Westport, CT: Praeger, 1995.

Ellie Lee, ed., *Abortion Law and Politics Today.* New York: St. Martin's, 1998.

Daniel C. Maguire, *Sacred Rights: The Case for Contraception and Abortion in World Religions.* New York: Oxford University Press, 2003.

Eileen McDonagh, *Breaking the Abortion Deadlock: From Choice to Consent.* New York: Oxford University Press, 1996.

Roy M. Mersky and Jill Duffy, eds., *A Documentary History of the Legal Aspects of Abortion in the United States.* Littleton, CO: Fred B. Rothman, 2000.

Lynn Marie Morgan and Meredith W. Michaels, eds., *Fetal Subjects, Feminist Positions.* Philadelphia: University of Pennsylvania Press, 1999.

Jennifer Nelson, *Women of Color and the Reproductive Rights Movement.* New York: New York University Press, 2003.

Rosemary Nosiff, *Before Roe: Abortion Policy in the States.* Philadelphia: Temple University Press, 2001.

Jerry Reiter, *Live from the Gates of Hell: An Insider's Look at the Anti-Abortion Movement.* Amherst, NY: Prometheus, 2000.

James Risen and Judy L. Thomas, *Wrath of Angels: The American Abortion War.* New York: BasicBooks, 1998.

Michael Roth, *Making Women Pay: The Hidden Costs of Fetal Rights.* Ithica, NY: Cornell University Press, 1999.

Kathy Rudy, *Beyond Pro-Life and Pro-Choice: Moral Diversity in the Abortion Debate.* Boston: Beacon, 1996.

William Saletan, *Bearing Right: How Conservatives Won the Abortion War.* Berkeley: University of California Press, 2003.

Alexander Sanger, *Beyond Choice: Reproductive Freedom in the Twenty-First Century.* New York: Public Affairs, 2004.

Rickie Solinger, ed., *Abortion Wars: A Half Century of Struggle, 1950–2000.* Berkeley: University of California Press, 1998.

Raymond Tatalovich, *The Politics of Abortion in the United States and Canada: A Comparative Study.* Armonk, NY: M.E. Sharpe, 1997.

Teresa R. Wagner, *Back to the Drawing Board: The Future of the Pro-Life Movement.* South Bend, IN: St. Augustine's, 2003.

Peter S. Wenz, *Abortion Rights as Religious Freedom.* Philadelphia: Temple University Press, 1992.

Web Sites

American Civil Liberties Union Reproductive Freedom Project, www.aclu.org. The American Civil Liberties Union is an organization that works to protect Americans' civil rights as guaranteed in the Bill of Rights. Its Freedom Project seeks to defend women's legal right to abortion. It disseminates fact sheets, pamphlets, and editorials.

Catholics for a Free Choice, www.cath4choice.org. The site of an organization that supports the right to legal abortion and promotes family planning to reduce the incidence of abortion and increase women's choices in childbearing and child rearing.

Human Life Foundation, www.humanlifereview.com. The human life foundation is a nonprofit organization that promotes alternatives to abortion. It provides grants to support crisis pregnancy centers nationwide and publishes the quarterly journal *Human Life Review* as well as books and pamphlets on abortion.

National Right to Life Committee, www.nrlc.org. The Web site of an organization that opposes abortion and advocates a constitutional amendment granting embryos and fetuses the same right to life as living persons. It promotes alternatives to abortion, such as adoption.

Operation Rescue, www.operationrescue.org. Operation Rescue formed in 1986 to conduct civil disobedience to protest abortion. Activists routinely blocked access to clinics in order to prevent women from obtaining abortions. Currently the organization operates in California, where it exposes abortion doctors in an effort to shut them down.

Planned Parenthood Federation of America, www.plannedpare nthood.org. The site of an organization that advocates people's right to make their own reproductive choices free from governmental control. The federation provides contraception, family planning, and abortion services at clinics across the United States.

INDEX